Should You Be The Working Mom?

SHOULD YOU BE THE WORKING MOM?

A GUIDE FOR MAKING THE DECISION AND LIVING WITH THE RESULTS

BEE-LAN C. WANG, PH.D.,
RICHARD J. STELLWAY, PH.D.

LIFEJOURNEY BOOKS

DAVID C. COOK PUBLISHING CO.
ELGIN, ILLINOIS—WESTON, ONTARIO

LifeJourney Books is an imprint of David C. Cook Publishing Co.

David C. Cook Publishing Co., Elgin, Illinois 60120
David C. Cook Publishing Co., Weston, Ontario

SHOULD YOU BE THE WORKING MOM?

Edited by Joan Lloyd Guest
Design by Chris Patchel
Photo by Bakstad Photographics

First Printing, 1987
Printed in the United States of America
92 91 90 89 88 87 5 4 3 2 1

Wang, Bee-Lan,
Should you be the working mom?/Bee-Lan Wang, Richard Stellway
p. cm.
Includes index.
ISBN 1-555-13322-3
1. Working mothers—United States. 2. Work and family—United States. I. Stellway, Richard, 1943— II. Title.
HQ759.48.W36 1987
306.8'7—dc19

87-20306
CIP

CONTENTS

ACKNOWLEDGMENTS

We are indebted to the following people for their parts in the process of writing this book:

Joan Lloyd Guest, our editor, whose skill, patience and hard work were invaluable in shaping the final product;

Paul Mouw, the managing editor of LifeJourney Books, whose vision gave birth to the idea for this book;

The many persons we interviewed, who shared their joys and sorrows, aspirations and fears with us; our spouses, Timothy and Betty, who acted as our harshest critics and our greatest encouragers; our children: Stephen, Jason, and Paul Wang, who started the habit of getting their own breakfasts while their mom was writing this book, and Kelley Stellway, who endured her dad's paying more attention to the computer than to her at times; and the St. Charles, Illinois, Public Library, whose children's department staff made the Wang boys feel very much at home those times when the reference staff was helping their mom with the research for this book.

It is our hope and prayer that this book will be of much help to both working and stay-at-home mothers (or mothers-to-be) and their families in many ways.

PART I

OUR CHANGING WORLD

INTRODUCTION:

CHOICES AND QUESTIONS

"Hey, Carol! How are you? I haven't seen you in a while. Are you working now?" Lucy was genuinely interested in Carol's news.

"What do you mean, am I working now?" Carol snapped spontaneously and then wondered at her response. She had been glad to see Lucy, but her remark didn't show it.

Carol lived with her husband and their two boys, aged 13 and 5, in a thriving suburb. Before their second child was born, Carol completed nursing school. She worked part-time after the baby came along. But she had recently quit her job to spend more time with her sons. Lucy's question hit a nerve.

Lucy and her husband were both active in church. Bob was an executive with a big corporation and traveled a lot. Lucy was a self-employed accountant. They had three young children.

Carol had always felt as though she couldn't live up to Lucy's standards. She liked and admired Lucy, but felt intimidated by all her activities. Now that Carol had quit work she felt even more insecure.

Tension, intimidation, conflicting expectations, and guilt seem to be common these days among mothers and their families. Those who don't work sometimes feel like failures because they are "just housewives." Those who do work often feel guilty because they don't spend as much time with their children as their at-home counterparts. And all kinds of women try to make up for their feelings by presenting their way of life as the only right way.

Redbook magazine conducted a survey not long ago on the question, Do kids need a stay-at-home mom? They were surprised at the responses they got.

> We hadn't expected the impassioned outpouring we received: letters five and six pages long . . . from coal miners' wives, aerobics instructors, licensed day-care operators, bankers, waitresses, accountants, teachers, farmers. Women . . . with anywhere from one child to . . . six, responded. Many said it was the first time they had ever written to a magazine.[1]

There seems to be more heat than light being generated by the question of working motherhood. Another popular women's magazine observed that "Women seemed to support one another throughout the 1970s in asserting their individual right to work or not to work. But, in the 1980s, if you are a mother, making a choice means having to defend that choice to everyone."[2]

This holds true for Christian mothers as well. In fact, the argument rages perhaps more fiercely among people who hold to biblical values. Scripture verses are quoted on both sides of the battle to justify absolute positions. Those who espouse working motherhood often refer to the woman of Proverbs 31—she ran a business, a household, and raised children. If she did it all, why shouldn't today's mom? Those who take the opposite view—that mothers should stay home to raise their kids—quote passages from the letters of Paul that suggest that women are to focus their energies on family-related duties.

In this book we will try to shed a little more light—without so much heat—on the subject of working and parenting. We want to help parents, especially mothers, make the choice of whether to work. And we want to help those who choose to or have to work to be successful at both tasks.

This book is organized into three parts. Part one will offer some biblical perspectives on work and women. We will also look at changes that have come about in our society and changes that may come in the future.

Part two will raise the difficult question: should I work or not? We will examine the issue of what it means to try to "have it all." Is money the main issue? Or is it personal satisfaction? Are there valid reasons for being a working mother or not? More importantly, what happens to the children when both parents work? Do they suffer or thrive or both? And what happens to the marriage?

Finally, part three will offer some practical suggestions for those mothers—and fathers—who choose to work: finding good substitute care, setting priorities, dealing with superhuman expectations.

No matter what we decide to do about work and parenting, we are bound to come across people who do not approve of our choices. There are two ways to handle such people.

One way is to turn up our noses at them. They are wrong; we are right. That's all there is to it. But this attitude neither makes for good relationships nor for learning and growing together. This attitude is just a defense mechanism. It puts us smack in the middle of the current battle between working and at-home mothers.

The other way of handling people who have chosen differently is to think through why they have made their choices and why we have made ours. One reason a battle rages between working mothers and those at home is that both sides have set up stereotypes of the other. All working mothers are supposed to be callous, overly ambitious women's libbers who have little regard for their children (and none at all for biblical values). All at-home mothers are supposed to be dull-witted, TV-watching women who get a great kick out of conquering waxy yellow buildup on the kitchen floor.

Of course, neither picture is accurate, and the more we can strip away the emotional wrappings and get to the real issues, the more capable we will be of making an informed decision about our own lives and feeling good about our choice.

In this book we want to be biblically based and well-informed. Bee-Lan Wang is an educator who has also been a working mother. She and her husband, Timothy, have three boys ranging in age from four to ten. Richard Stellway is a professor of sociology and his wife, Betty, is a bank secretary. They have a sixteen-year-old daughter. Both authors are committed to putting Christ first in our lives and in our families. Our desire is to offer insight and relevant facts to women and men who face one of today's most difficult choices.

One important note on style: While Richard Stellway contributed ideas throughout the book, Bee-Lan Wang did all the writing except for chapters six and ten. Thus, "I" refers to Bee-Lan except in chapters six and ten where "I" refers to Richard.

1

WOMEN AND WORK

CHANGES ALWAYS AROUSE CONTROVERSY. OVER THE last twenty years women in America have gone back to work by the millions. And our society is struggling to both accommodate and justify that trend. It seems to be a trend that's here to stay.

This chart shows the percentage of mothers in the labor force (either working or looking for work).[1]

	Age of Youngest Child				
	1 or under	2 yrs.	4 yrs.	6 yrs.	10 yrs.
1970	24%	30.5%	39%	44%	49%
1975	31	37	41	47	57
1985	49	54	60	64.5	68

These figures include only married wives living with their husbands. Single mothers tend to work outside the home at rates about equal to those of married women when their children are very young. After age six, however, single mothers tend to work more.

When women started coming out to work in numbers that attracted national attention, in about 1970, they typically did so only after their youngest child had reached age twelve. In 1975 the majority of mothers waited until their youngest child was in school. By 1985, however, the majority were back at work by the time their youngest was age two. Moreover, the vast majority of mothers who work do so full-time.

Why has this trend developed? Why are so many more women working when their children are very young? One reason is that many of these are working women who postponed childbearing while they established careers. They were working and childless in the 1970s. Then in the 1980s they began to have children and to return to their careers shortly afterward.

There was a mini baby boom in the early 1980s. But in 1986 the birthrate in America reached an all-time low. It might be that many of these children born in mid-career will end up being the only children in their families.

Lisa is one of those women who had their first babies in the early 1980s. She and Jonathan met while in college. They both had strong commitments to careers and made long-term plans to support each other in their respective fields when they got married after graduation.

Jonathan went to journalism school after college, and she trained as a physician's assistant. She worked for two years, finished a master's degree in the sociology of health, and then was accepted into medical school. By then Jon had obtained an MBA and started a career with a publishing company. They had been married five years when they planned their first child to arrive the summer after her first year in medical school. Gaylen was born in 1983.

Lisa took a year off to be with Gaylen. After she went back to school, Jon became his primary care giver, along with two women who were paid to baby-sit during the day. Now Lisa has graduated and they are wondering when to have their second child.

As more and more women like Lisa have become committed to both career and family, the women's movement has changed its emphasis to the area of family concerns. And well it should. The typical family today has two incomes, and women are struggling under dual sets of responsibilities. By helping them, we are helping not just working mothers, but fathers and children also.

Help Overdue

American women are behind their counterparts in other industrialized countries when it comes to help for the working mother. In France, women are entitled to a minimum of sixteen weeks of maternity leave at 84 percent of their pay. Sweden pays new moms 90 percent of their salaries for six months after childbirth while fathers, too, are guaranteed extensive leaves of absence. Israel provides new mothers with twelve weeks of paid leave and forty weeks of unpaid leave. In Japan, although most mothers quit work when their babies come, women are entitled to fourteen weeks of maternity leave.[2]

These same countries also tend to provide more help for fathers and mothers when it comes to child care. In many industrialized countries, publicly subsidized day care is available, although demand still exceeds supply. France also provides a subsidy of up to $340 for parents who hire help in the home.

By contrast, in the U.S. there are few protections and almost no benefits for working mothers. The Pregnancy Discrimination Act was passed in 1978. It protects women affected by childbirth, pregnancy, and related medical conditions from being fired or refused a job or promotion. It requires that pregnancy be treated as any other temporary medical disability and covered by sick pay and insurance when those are available. Unfortunately, however, many employers do not provide such benefits or do not provide them to those who work part-time. (And it is always difficult to prove that discrimination against a woman has taken place when other reasons can easily be given for a termination or a refusal to hire.)

Also, this bill only provides for pregnancy and childbirth as a medical condition. It protects a woman only for that period of time during which a doctor says she is unable to work (usually six weeks in the case of a normal birth). It does not take into account that childbirth is also a major life event. It fails to come to grips with the need for mothers to spend time with their infants. And, of course, it does not at all provide for new fathers.

One bill that was introduced in the U.S. Congress would require businesses employing fifteen or more persons to provide eighteen weeks of *unpaid* leave for the birth, adoption, or critical illness of a child. During this time medical insurance would be continued. The bill would also guarantee reinstatement to the employee's original or equivalent position following such a leave.

If legislation like this became law perhaps fewer mothers would rush back to work before they or their children were physically or psychologically ready. But at present only a minority of women in a few states are entitled to lengthier, unpaid maternity leave. And only those few women who work for companies which provide disability pay or allow sick time to be accrued over long periods are able to take maternity leave with pay. There are no benefits at all for men.

Men who take "paternity leave," usually only those who enjoy a great deal of independence in their jobs, are faced with incredulous employers and colleagues. They can lose the esteem of co-workers and clients for putting family concerns before their work. At present they can also lose their jobs. Thus, with rare exceptions, it is only the woman who takes maternity leave and only the mother who stays home when a child is sick.

Slowly, the U.S. government and businesses may be recognizing that two-income families are typical and that such families struggle to balance jobs and child rearing. The tax laws now allow families to deduct a proportion of the income spent on child care. And businesses can also take deductions for child-care assistance provided to employees. However, such provisions for families are still minimal.

Some three to four thousand companies now offer some kind of child-care help. Some of these, including Proctor and

Gamble and Campbell's, have begun day-care centers. (But the excessive cost of liability insurance for centers has discouraged many businesses from trying this and has forced some on-the-job, day-care centers to close.) Other companies, such as IBM, offer day-care referral services. Yet these companies still represent only a very small number of workers in this country.

Discomfort

Perhaps one reason why progress in favor of working parents has been so slow is that American society is still very ambivalent about the growing numbers of working mothers. While some laws have been passed and some men have become liberated enough to be active fathers and supportive husbands of working wives, there is still not enthusiastic help for working mothers.

In a recent survey of over 2000 families, 74 percent felt that a mother with a young child should not work unless there was true financial hardship.[3] In another survey, 75 percent of at-home mothers agreed with the statement, "When a mother works outside the home, her children almost always suffer."[4]

But what about working mothers themselves—how would they respond to that statement? Here's where the surprise comes in. *Half* of the working mothers also agreed with that statement. Yet the majority of mothers with young children are working today. And of those who work, nearly two-thirds do so full-time. Many of them must, therefore, feel guilty for doing so since they believe their children will suffer.

And the guilt is laid on them from outside as well as within. When at-home mothers were asked why other mothers work, 39 percent responded that these other women work because they don't want to take care of their children. But the facts don't add up. If these women didn't want to take care of children why would they have children in the first place? Women are truly divided over the issue of working and motherhood. A lot of finger pointing is going on.

Many of the accusations today arise from concern over what is happening to the American family. Certainly we should be concerned. We should be concerned enough to take a close look at what fathers, as well as mothers, are doing. We have high ideals for our families, and we should. Unfortunately, reality often just doesn't match the ideal. For example, in one survey 91 percent of the respondents said that fathers should spend as much time with their children as mothers.[5] Yet how many families come even close to that ideal? Can you think of one? Study after study has shown that even in two-career families, mothers inevitably spend more time with their children than fathers.

The divorce rate is used on both sides to justify particular views. Many people suggest that because so many children will face the prospect of their parents' divorce, they need to have a full-time, at-home parent. Yet a twelve-year study has shown that women who feel insecure in their marriages are *more* likely to join the labor force than those who feel secure. Because they expect or fear divorce, they want to plan for their own financial independence. The instability of marriage is therefore one overlooked cause of the rise of women in the work force, not the other way around.[6]

The state of her marriage, money, the condition of her home, the welfare of her children—all these are issues facing the working mother. Her own psychological and emotional health is at stake, especially given the strong crosscurrents of public opinion about working mothers. Such opinions surface even in everyday conversations between friends.

What Is Work?

One woman reported a conversation with a male friend, Dennis, an insurance executive. "Dennis told me I shouldn't be out working. I should stay home and be with my children. We could learn to live on less, he said. Money isn't everything." This woman is a part-time bank teller while her husband is a carpenter.

"I know money isn't everything," she continued. "But just because I'm working that doesn't mean I'm not taking good care of my kids. Look at Dennis' wife. She's got lots of money so she doesn't have to work for pay. But she doesn't even have time to take her kids swimming. The baby-sitter does that."

One woman works. The other doesn't. Or does she? Dennis' wife is very involved in community activities and volunteer jobs. So what is work anyway?

The mother who does not bring home a paycheck, but spends her time cleaning, sewing, driving the children to soccer games and dental checkups, arranging swimming and music lessons and cooking—doesn't she also work? What about the wife who helps her husband in his business? Should she stop doing that so she can be fully available to their children?

Or what about Sophia, a school board member? One day another woman said to her, "You should quit being so busy with the school district and take care of your children."

An older lady heard this and said, "She is not only taking care of her own children, she is taking care of thousands of other children, including yours!"

Perhaps work, however defined, is not the real issue. Perhaps it is a matter of priorities and perspectives. And not just women's priorities but also men's—the whole family's.

Is it right that most fathers spend so little time with their families? Is it right that financial and job success is counted so much more important for men than success at being an attentive parent?

The question of proper priorities arises with both men and women. And it comes up not just with paid employment but with other activities as well. What is happening to friendship in this day when everyone is busy earning a living? What about the simple joys of gardening or taking walks? of keeping up with extended family members? of finding joy in a hobby?

These questions posed themselves to me one day as I was rushing out the door, unable to stay long enough to talk to the baby-sitter who was having personal problems and obviously needed a friend that day. What big project was taking me so hastily out of the house? Writing this book!

These days organizations that rely heavily on volunteer help are having a difficult time. Many churches have had to end programs like summer Vacation Bible School because they can't find people to run them. The women who used to do so have all gone back to work.

One time I conducted a survey at church asking for volunteers for the children's worship program. One couple answered, "We can't help. We have a baby." Wasn't that just the reason why I needed their help? Their baby and others required care. Then I realized that the real reason they could not help was that they both held demanding jobs. Even when their child got older they were never available for volunteer work at church.

In *Parents and Children* Anthony Campolo writes, "The two-career family is here to stay. The person who stays in the pulpit simplistically saying, 'The wife ought to stay home and only the husband ought to work,' belongs to another generation." Is he right? Certainly the two-earner family is now typical and seems to be here to stay. But is that the way things should be?

This book is not designed to answer that question for you. But we hope here to be able to help you make up your own mind on this issue. We want to help you sort through the confusion and guilt and get to the heart of the matter. We want to provide you with facts about working and parenting. We want to share our own experiences and research and those of others so that you can better understand your options, deal with your feelings, and sort through your priorities. We want to help you to decide how you can best fulfill God's desires for your life and your family.

We will also offer some practical guidelines for families that decide to try to balance work and parenting. And we will speak to fathers about their role in the family.

Expectations and demands will always confront you, frequently causing conflict. There is no escaping your responsibilities in this society. You need to decide which demands and expectations you will meet and which you will not. And having decided, you need to figure out how to best balance all the needs that you and those around you have.

2

SHOULD MOTHERS HAVE JOBS?

"I JUST LOVE CLEANING HOUSES," PEGGY SAID.

Sue looked at her in disbelief. Has she managed to persuade herself into this attitude, thought Sue, out of necessity?

"Man may work from sun to sun, but woman's work is never done," Sue quoted to Peggy. Sue thought housecleaning the most unrewarding work because it always had to be done over again. It always seemed to be a losing battle.

Sue had been following Peggy around on this first day that Peggy cleaned for her. She kept telling Peggy not to put so much effort on the less used corners of the home. Sue did not feel comfortable that Peggy was polishing even the underside of her toddler's piggy bank. But here was Peggy telling Sue that she loved cleaning houses.

Sue soon came to see that Peggy was a very unusual housecleaner. Peggy really did love cleaning. She did a far better job than any other person Sue knew. Each time after Peggy was through, Sue's husband would take a deep breath when he came home and say, "Wow, this place smells really clean!"

Why did Peggy like housecleaning? "I use the time to talk with the Lord," she told Sue. She usually had a radio on or else listened to a tape of some Bible message while she cleaned. But that did not completely explain her enthusiasm.

Several months later, Peggy was talking to Sue about church and opportunities for service to God. "What do you mean when you say 'service to God'?" Sue asked.

"Why, everything that I do," Peggy replied. "Raising my kids, cooking for my family, teaching Sunday school, everything."

Paul wrote to the Ephesians, "Serve wholeheartedly, as if you were serving the Lord, not men" (6:7). Paul was addressing a particular group of people, but we would all be better off if we could take his advice. What a difference it would make if we brought this attitude to everything we do, from wiping little noses to running a corporation. Work is ordained by the Lord. To each person, at each given time and place, God has given a certain set of tasks to accomplish.

In Genesis we read that after God made Adam and Eve, He said to them, "Be fruitful and increase in number; fill the earth and subdue it. Rule over the fish of the sea and the birds of the air and over every living creature that moves on the ground" (Gen. 1:28). God took Adam "and put him in the Garden of Eden to work it and take care of it" (Gen. 2:15). He then made Eve as a "helper suitable for him" (Gen. 2:18).

Work is something that God ordained for men and women to do right from the start, even before the Fall. Work is our partnership with God. He made this world, and we are to tend it. Work was not to cause painful toil or sweat. Pain and sweat were, instead, part of the punishment for Adam and Eve's disobedience (Gen. 3:17-19).

There are, of course, many different kinds of work. Changing diapers and mopping floors, operating on damaged kidneys and managing pension funds, painting walls and performing a piece of music—all these are work. There is work that brings in a paycheck and work that does not. There is work that stacks up into what is known as a career, and there is work that seems to lead nowhere. There is work that is obligatory and work that is voluntary. But these are all work.

Whatever God has given us to do, if we do it with the attitude that we are serving Him, it will be work that gives a sense of satisfaction in its accomplishment. For mothers who wonder whether to work to bring home a paycheck or to take care of the family full-time, this understanding should enable us to view our options in the correct perspective.

How Families Have Changed

The question of whether a mother should take on paid employment was not an issue in previous societies. That question has, rather, become an issue because of the structure of today's industrialized society. A lot of things are different for today's parents than they were for previous generations.

First, in this country today there is a much higher degree of separation between family life and work life. In agricultural societies people generally do not go away from home to work. Even when they do, their children often go with them.

When American society was primarily rural, work and leisure were not so clearly distinguished as they are today. Work was part of the warp and woof of most homes, interwoven within the daily routine of living and family relationships. Every member of farm families, other than the very youngest, contributed to the chores of the home, taking care of the animals and the needs of the land.

Before factories and mass production, the economic activities of many nonfarm families, too, took place in or near the home. Shoes, clothes, lumber, and other products were often made or processed at home. Or perhaps the home doubled as the corner store. In these situations, fathers did not have to leave the house in the morning and not return until evening in order to do their work. Mothers did not ask whether they should be involved in economically gainful activity.

I grew up in a home that was also a bakery. My mother, a widow, did not run the business. My aunt did. Her husband had an office job (unusual in those days), and she had the bakery. My mom worked for my aunt while at the same time acting as the landlady for the building. As I grew older, I helped with the baking. I rolled cookie dough, mixed sugar and flour, and cut cakes. I was also the "garbage can" for rejects out of the oven—a role I enjoyed very much!

A second difference between today's families and yesterday's is that nuclear families are now the norm. As families have become more mobile, fewer of us are able to enjoy the benefits of having relatives living nearby. The fortunate few who do can take advantage of an informal exchange of service among relatives even if they do not live under the same roof.

Helen is one of these fortunate ones. She taught school when her youngest child, Becky, was still a preschooler. The car pool used to take Becky to her grandmother after school, and Helen would pick Becky up on her way home from work. Today, Becky is in college and has a wonderful relationship both with her parents and grandparents. Grandma and Becky remember well her favorite lunch, chicken noodle soup, and Becky's pretenses at taking a nap each afternoon when she was really playing house on Grandma's big bed.

The combination of the rise of the nuclear family and the separation of work from family life has led to a third reason why mothers' employment is now an issue: specialization within the family. Once the process of making a living moved out of the household, it ceased to be "everybody's business." In our economy of mass production, big companies and service occupations, the family now functions only as a unit of consumption, not an economically productive unit. Since the entire family can no longer participate in the task of earning a living, the job has been delegated to one particular member—Dad. Dad has gone out of the house to work while Mom has stayed home to take care of the family. At least that's the way things were until about fifteen years ago.

During that time, a set of norms and values—a belief system if you will—grew up to affirm this way of life. It's that system of values that is thrown into question when mothers begin to work outside the home. That's perhaps why this issue about working mothers raises so many conflicting emotions. It calls into doubt values which have become basic to our American way of life.

What About Dads?

Conspicuous in this whole discussion is the lack of question about the role of men. No one asks whether fathers should work outside the home because the task of producing income has been allocated to fathers. There is nothing wrong with this division of labor. We need to understand, however, that such a division is arbitrary. There is no law—natural, divine, or man-made—that says that mothers cannot help provide financially for the family, or that fathers should not also be nurturers of their children. In fact, problems arise when we assume that the only role a father plays is to provide income. A man is not being a good father when he spends almost all of his time and energies making money.

We frequently hear, "Children need their mothers." But it's rare to hear, "Children need their fathers." Yet they do. Research studies seem to show that more homosexuals come from families where the father was either not often present or did not have a warm relationship with his children. Many of these emotionally distant fathers were considered good dads because they were skilled at financially providing for their families. But their children suffered in spite of it.

On the other extreme, we sometimes feel that if a man cannot make enough money to meet his family's financial goals, then he is not a fit father. But this is a statement about the market for this man's skills, not a statement about his fatherhood. Should he take time away from his family in order to hold a second job and provide more money? Or should he go around feeling like less of a man because his family lives in an apartment instead of owning a house?

Kate bought into this idea that the man should be the one to provide for all the family's financial needs. Three years after she and Bill were married, a child came along. She quit her grocery store job and took on housecleaning jobs so her toddler could be with her. But one day her young son broke an expensive vase in a home she was cleaning. In a rage, she called Bill at work: "Your son just broke a valuable vase. What are you going to do about it?"

Kate's anger arose in part from the fact that she blamed Bill for not being able to provide for the family. She didn't want to work and felt that it should have been her privilege not to—after all, making money is the man's responsibility. Kate worked only because Bill's paycheck didn't pay all the bills. Is that why most women work these days?

Why Women Work

The last three decades have seen a dramatic increase in the number of wives and mothers in paid employment. Why is this? One reason is education. More women now are high-school or college graduates than were in the 1950s. And the more highly educated a woman is, the more likely she is to work or to want to work. A more educated woman will find it easier to locate a job that is both financially and personally rewarding. She will also be more likely to feel a need for interests outside the home.

Before we blame the trend on education, however, we must remember that most women who work do so for monetary reasons. In 1975, an income of just under $10,000 was required for a family of four to enjoy a low standard of living. At that time 9.5 million of the 37 million women in the labor force were married to men who earned less than $10,000 per year. Another 7 million working women were widowed, divorced, or separated and therefore provided their families' primary income. These women worked out of necessity.

Other women, however, work for financial reasons, but not because their families would go hungry without their work. Their husbands make enough money to pay all the bills, but the second income provides an added measure of comfort. In 1984, the median income of two-earner families was $32,711. This was half again as much as the figure for families in which the wife did not work ($21,911).

For many families, the extra income is what allows them to

own their own home. The median price of a new single-family home doubled from 1965 to 1975 and doubled again from 1975 to 1984. In 1965 a new house cost, on average, $20,000. In 1984 that price had increased to almost $80,000.[1] While price increases have varied from region to region, the fact is that the American dream of owning a home is often no longer realizable for one-income families.

When Jennifer and Jim moved out to California from the Midwest with their two preschoolers, Jennifer had to go back to working full-time. She was a nurse and had been working two nights per week prior to their move. Even though they had built up some equity in their first home by the time they sold it, prices in the San Francisco area were way too high for them to pay their mortgage from just one paycheck.

Being able to afford a home depends not only on the price of the home, but to a large extent on the size of the monthly payments. The latter vary with interest rates. When interest rates are high, it takes a larger income to qualify for a mortgage than when interest rates are low. The early 1980s saw record-high interest rates. Families who had been saving to buy their first homes then found that they could no longer afford it. Some mothers went back to work out of frustration with having their dream of home ownership deferred.

But what other factors have sent mothers into the working world? Many cite personal satisfaction. Fran, for example, returned to work when her daughter was three. She and Mike seemed to "have it all." Mike was an insurance salesman, and they had a three-bedroom home on a large lot outside a small city. Their daughter, with her head of curly hair, was a darling. Fran loved her dearly and liked seeing her grow up.

But Fran got bored with her daily routine. You can only put together so many Disney puzzles and read so many Richard Scarry stories before the tasks begin to grow tiresome. Fran started to feel very isolated in her rural home. So she decided to try her hand at the real estate business, working three days per week. She found the challenge rejuvenating. On her days off she enjoyed her daughter more because their time together was more limited. She was also able to afford a second car, so she wasn't as isolated when she wasn't working.

Fran's situation is typical of many women today. They need adult company, and they need to get out of the house. Mothers of young children can be quite isolated, especially in suburban or rural areas or in harsh climates.

Yet many people who hold to more traditional values criticize mothers who feel a need for outlets outside the home. They believe that such women are simply being selfish. But perhaps that begs the question. The real issue is whether a woman with outside responsibilities can do a good job of parenting. And the answer here is not an obvious no.

Studies indicate that the best mothers and fathers are those who are happiest with their lives. Thus, a mother who is frustrated and dissatisfied at home may take out her frustrations on her children, just as the father who is unhappy at work may bring his problems home with him. By the same token, a woman who has to work but does not want to may have trouble being a patient and loving parent. The question is one of peace and happiness, not work per se.

Many women have a deep need to perform tasks more challenging than changing diapers or pushing children on the backyard swing. In fact, these feelings of isolation and lack of fulfillment were some of the basic issues which arose in the early days of the women's movement. Betty Friedan first described these feelings in *The Feminine Mystique* as "the problem that has no name."

It's not clear exactly why so many more women have become discontented with their lives in recent decades. Part of the problem may be the women's movement itself. Women's expectations have risen, as has the pressure to do something other than be "just a wife and mother." But the nature of motherhood has also changed. Mothers at home have more leisure time and less of a community supporting them in their role at home. Motherhood is not the sacred profession that it once was, and the working world has gained a glamor that it previously lacked. So more mothers are choosing to try to do both—to raise their children and to work. Are they right or wrong?

Is There a Biblical Answer?

Some influential preachers say categorically that Christian mothers must stay home with their children. These ministers lay at the doorstep of working mothers all types of modern problems such as divorce and teen suicide. A mother who is out working is clearly doing something sinful, we are told. But is the issue that clear?

The Bible makes few, if any, direct statements about this issue. It's clear that children are to be valued and treated with love and respect. Parents are to instruct their children in the Word, to discipline them and to treat each other with love and submission. But the Good Book says little about the specifics of parenting and working, other than prohibitions on certain sinful types of work such as stealing and prostitution. Instead, we're given general principles and a few examples of biblical parenthood.

One example frequently cited as a model for Christian womanhood is the woman of Proverbs 31. This woman and her activities are described in some detail. And she was a busy woman! A brief list of her characteristics would include:

- she is married (vs. 10)
- her husband trusts her fully (vs. 11)
- she is good for her husband (vs. 12)
- she spins and works with her hands (vs. 13)
- she purchases supplies from distant sources (vs. 14)
- she provides food for her household (vs. 15)
- she is prosperous and has servants (vs. 15)
- she invests in real estate and engages in commercial agriculture (financed out of her own earnings) (vs. 16)
- she works hard, sleeps little and is strong (vss. 15, 17, 18)
- she trades for profit (vs. 18)

- she does charitable work (vs. 20)
- members of her household dress well (vs. 21)
- her home is well decorated (vs. 21)
- her husband is a respected leader (vs. 23)
- she is involved in manufacturing (vs. 24)
- she is prepared for the future (vs. 25)
- she is wise and teaches others (vs. 26)
- she diligently administers her household affairs (vs. 27)
- her children and husband appreciate her (vss. 28, 29)

Rather than prohibiting mothers from engaging in activities that in this society are male strongholds—investing, commerce, agriculture—Scripture lauds a mother who does all this and still provides well for the everyday needs of her family.

Verses 30 and 31 indicate the motivation behind this woman's achievements: "Charm is deceptive, and beauty is fleeting; but a woman who fears the Lord is to be praised." Her accomplishments are not mere appearances, nor are they made for the purpose of winning human accolades. They arise, instead, out of a fear of the Lord which leads to faithful service in whatever she has to do.

Is every Christian woman supposed to try to mimic this superwoman's accomplishments? No. This passage is not a prescription for our lives. But it describes an ideal. More importantly, it encourages all women to be productive in all kinds of earthly labors. It enjoins women (and men) to fear the Lord, to obey His commands, and to serve Him faithfully by serving others.

This does not mean that every mother should rush out to take on a job in real estate or nursing. But we are not to automatically close those doors either. The Proverbs 31 woman gained praise in the sight of God even though she had involvements and interests outside her home and children. Perhaps that is the main message. We should keep an open mind to the opportunities for service which God may bring our way—at home or outside the home, paying or "voluntary." The important thing is that whatever we choose to do should be for His glory, not ours. The Lord will provide the resources for the work He gives us, and He will reward faithful service.

PART II

MAKING THE CHOICE

3

CHILDREN OR CAREER?

WHY DO PEOPLE TODAY HAVE CHILDREN? IN SOME countries around the world, the reasons for having children are still the same today as they were centuries ago—children provide help for the family, extra income perhaps, and security for old age.

But in industrialized countries today the reasons for having children have changed. Children do not help produce food for the family. Pensions take care of aging parents. And high mobility often keeps families from seeing each other once the children are grown. So the reasons for having children are now related much more to intangible things like love and emotional desire.

A mother of five told us, "Children triple love." Others say that children provide opportunities for "sharing, communicating and caring." They "teach you to be unselfish and patient." These sentiments match the findings of a major study conducted some ten years ago by University of Hawaii researchers. They found that Americans primarily valued children as sources of "happiness, love, and companionship." Also, couples see children as sources of personal challenge and growth. And parents desire the opportunity to instill values in their children.[1]

The Motherhood Report, a nationwide study of 1,100 mothers, quotes one woman as saying, "Before I had a baby I always dreamed of making a valuable contribution to the world. . . . When my child was a baby I knew that this was it. I would never be as important to someone as I was right then. You are the center of the child's universe."[2]

Those words echo the feelings of many mothers. Yet others hold a different view. They recognize that along with the center of the universe come dirty diapers, baby bottles and burnt dinners. Yet such sentiments are difficult to express in a country where motherhood has been elevated to the status of sainthood. It's almost against the law in America to say anything bad about motherhood.

The Motherhood Report states that seven out of ten women admitted they had romantic notions of motherhood before they had children. They expected child raising to be a blissful experience with few real difficulties. Many expected to be ideal mothers. Most women vowed they would never spank or spoil their children—or lose control. These women—and they were the majority—were wrong. Most mothers spank their kids, and virtually all lose their tempers from time to time. This romanticized notion of parenting has not done justice to the reality.[3] And reality is what women must face when they consider whether to try to combine a career with motherhood.

In this chapter we would like to look at some of the key sacrifices that must be made when children and careers are considered. We will look at the extremes—sacrificing career or sacrificing childbearing—and their consequences and alternatives.

Bearing and raising children are among the greatest privileges and the greatest responsibilities anyone can have. You receive a lot from your children, especially if they "turn out right." You also must give a lot. The Bible recognizes children as a gift from God and a blessing (e.g., Gen. 33:5; Ps. 127; Ps. 128). Perhaps Christ's words about giving are especially appropriate for talking about children: "Give, and it will be given to you. A good measure, pressed down, shaken together and running over, will be poured into your lap. For with the measure you use, it will be measured to you" (Lk 6:38). Children offer tremendous blessings, but only after tremendous sacrifice in time, sleep, leisure, money, success, and careers.

Opting for Childlessness

Recognizing the huge sacrifices that children require, some couples have chosen to remain childless. Prior to 1960, voluntary childlessness was almost unheard of. A 1961 study of college women found that only one percent preferred to remain childless. But in 1986 *Newsweek* reported that "the current overall rates of childlessness are the highest since the end of the Depression, but for very different reasons." Of women aged 35 to 39, about 15 per cent were childless in 1985.[4] Some of these are not childless by choice, but there are many more voluntarily childless couples today than a decade or two ago.

Is voluntary childlessness an option for Christian couples? That has always been a difficult question. There is little direct teaching on family planning in Scripture. Of course, there is good reason for that. Effective family planning was not even possible until about two generations ago. So, as it is on genetic engineering, computer technology and other modern issues, the Bible is silent on intentional childlessness. But there are relevant Scripture references that we can consider in context to see if they also apply today.

"Be fruitful and multiply." The first time that statement occurred was after God had created the birds and water creatures (Gen. 1:22). He told them to multiply. The second time God said that it was to Adam and Eve (Gen. 1:28). The third time He uttered such words was when He told Noah to bring the animals out after the great flood "so they can multiply on the earth" (Gen. 8:17). In all these situations it was especially necessary for the living creatures to multiply in order to survive.

God made similar statements to Jacob, who was the essential link in God's promise to Abraham that all the nations of the earth would be blessed through him. The nation of Israel and the Messiah came from Jacob's descendants.

It seems that "be fruitful and multiply" is perhaps not a command for all people at all times. Rather, it was a command appropriate to Old Testament times. The society in those days had a bias toward having children, as most primitive societies do. Children were blessings like arrows in a quiver (Ps. 127:5). They helped to obtain food and fend off enemies. Both for economic and military reasons, having children was a moral and patriotic duty. Owing to high death rates among infants and young children, many births were needed to ensure the survival of the race.

Times, of course, have changed. Modern medicine and a stable food base now enable the vast majority of our children to survive to adulthood. By contrast, overpopulation in some areas, pollution and resource scarcity can threaten human survival. In some countries concern for human welfare seems to dictate limits on childbearing rather than the other way around. (Although a negative birthrate can indeed adversely affect national stability and economic growth.)

In the New Testament, Jesus teaches about matters of marriage and divorce. But He nowhere speaks about a necessity to bear children. In fact, one of His few relevant statements is a warning that some mothers will regret having children because of the impending destruction of Jerusalem (Lk 23:29). At another point, when His listeners begin to elevate motherhood, He teaches that motherhood is less important than obeying God's will (Lk 11:27, 28).

Among Paul's writings, I Timothy 2:15 says that "women will be saved through childbearing." This verse is sometimes interpreted to mean that married women are required to have children. But a study of this and a related passage indicates that the intent of Paul's statement is to instruct women in avoiding temptation. In I Timothy 2:9-15 and I Timothy 5:3-16 Paul directs his teaching explicitly toward women. He tells younger widows to "marry, to have children, to manage their homes and to give the enemy no opportunity for slander" (v. 14). He also instructs women to show hospitality, help those in trouble and perform other good deeds.

Paul seems to be concerned that some women, because they did not have enough to do, were going from house to house gossiping and being busybodies. And he was concerned that some young widows might yield to sexual temptation if they did not remarry. So he teaches them to keep themselves busy with families and with doing good deeds. Thus they would be saved or "kept safe" through having children and continuing in faith, love, and holiness with propriety (2:15).

In these passages Paul is aiming to keep women from sinning by keeping them from idleness. In I Corinthians 7, by contrast, he encourages both men and women to remain single so that they will not be burdened by family responsibilities. In this chapter he makes clear that he believes that unmarried people are better able to give undivided devotion to God since they do not have to worry about pleasing their spouses.

Carrying this reasoning a little farther, one could speculate that in modern times Paul might counsel some married couples to remain childless so that they could more single-mindedly serve their Lord. Such an interpretation of I Corinthians 7 does not contradict the I Timothy passages if one remembers that Paul's intent in both passages is to help individuals put Christ and His concerns first in their lives. Paul wants us to make life's most important decisions in ways that will help rather than hinder us from being obedient to God and His ministry.

In some churches these days, there are childless married couples who are highly active and responsible members. They use their extra time to serve others. By contrast, we heard one mother remark that children provide an easy excuse for saying no to requests for help in church affairs! Which attitude is the more godly—those who remain childless and use their time in service or those who use their kids as a reason not to serve? The morality of this issue seems to lie in one's motivation and priorities. It's not a simple question of kids or no kids.

Parenthood should be something we enter into deliberately, soberly, and realistically, out of a desire to do all things for the glory of God. We should not become parents because we think society expects us to do so. Our first priority is to live our lives for God, and that might include a variety of different life-styles—married or single, childless or with children, employed outside the home or not.

With that said, however, we should also not romanticize Christian childlessness. If couples choose to remain childless out of dedication to God, they must recognize the sacrifice they may be making in personal satisfaction and companionship. It is still true that children help to provide for their parents in their old age. Childless couples (or more commonly, widows) face possible loneliness and destitution if they have no family willing to care for them. They need to make other arrangements for themselves as they get older.

Childless couples may face a good deal of regret as they approach middle age without the joys that children can bring. They will not see Johnny play oboe in the school recital, and they won't be able to applaud as Cindy accepts a medal for the 100-yard dash. They won't have anyone in their lives that they can influence in the way that parents can (or can try to!) influence their children.

If their decision was directed by God, however, they will have other rewards—perhaps the reward of watching spiritual children grow up in the Christian faith. God will not leave childless couples without comfort if they have faithfully served Him.

Opting Out of a Career

If, after weighing all the alternatives, couples choose to have children, then they must be prepared for the sacrifices that entails. If both parents have jobs, then *both* need to face the likelihood that their careers will in some way be compromised by the coming of children.

We tend to expect women to make compromises to balance a job and children. But men need to face that as well. If only the wife makes the sacrifices for the children, then there is something wrong in the family. A father cannot spend sixty to eighty hours or more per week away from home and still fulfill his responsibility as a father to "Impress [God's laws] on your children. Talk about them when you sit at home and when you walk along the road, when you lie down and when you get up" (Deut 6:7).

John is a father who takes the task of being a parent keenly to heart. He is an engineer with a large corporation. He and Ruth married when they were both in their thirties. They have one son. Ruth, who was a secretary before marrying, is now a full-time homemaker. Nevertheless, John does not leave all the home responsibilities to Ruth. Among other things they do as a family, John and Ruth set aside Friday evenings to spend on special activities with their son, Troy. And because John's present job takes him out of town a lot, he is looking for one that will require less travel. "It's not fair to Ruth and Troy that I am gone overnight so often," he says.

Another couple, convinced that the children needed a stay-at-home parent, went further. Husband and wife traded roles! Wife went to work full-time while Dad stayed at home. Hakon Torjesen, the dad, writes of his experiences in *The Househusband.*[5]

It is rare to find such fatherly attentiveness. It is even rarer to find a man who thinks as much of his wife's career as he does his own. Society does not regard such men highly. *The Wall Street Journal* carried an article about a man who stayed home for three years to care for children while his wife completed medical school.[6] When he was ready to return to work, he faced a grim reality: "There isn't a male I know of in an executive position who would accept raising kids as a legitimate excuse for not working for three years."

Why Women Make Compromises

The reality of the situation is that women make most of the sacrifices. There are several reasons for this. First, society (as this story pointed out) does not accept men who make sacrifices for families. In the movie *Kramer vs. Kramer,* the father is cross-examined by his wife's lawyer in a difficult custody battle. The attorney brings out the fact that Ted Kramer lost his previous, prestigious job due to "irresponsibility." That is supposed to show his unfitness as a father. In fact, he missed appointments with key clients because as a single parent he had to leave work to take care of a sick son. Parenting responsibilities aren't supposed to count when you are the father.

Women are given a little more leeway when it comes to the demands of being a working parent. But problems arise for women, too. Some bosses simply expect working mothers to do poorer work. When I requested a return to full-time status from part-time when my children were older, I was told, "This job requires 120 percent. You are a wife and mother—can you really give that much?" Many women can identify with that statement. They've heard it all before. But, as a society we should question if *any* job should require 120 percent, not whether a working mother can give it.

For men, marriage is an asset to their careers, not a source of conflict. And children are a pleasure, not a burden (unless fatherhood is taken too "seriously"). Sylvia Hewlett, author of *A Lesser Life—The Myth of Women's Liberation in America,* states, "If you look at 40-year-old, successful professional women who have stayed on track, only 35 to 40 percent of them have had a child. And yet 93 percent of their male colleagues have reached the same position and have families."[6]

A second reason why in many families the choice is made to sacrifice the mother's career, not the father's, is because mother earns less than father. Despite apparent progress for women, the fact remains that women earn only 68 cents for every dollar a man makes. Laws to prevent exploitation of women, especially those in typically female occupations like secretary and bank clerk, have failed to win passage because of the difficulty of determining "comparable worth." So few families can even consider letting the husband quit work instead of the wife because they could not afford the loss of his larger income.

Third, biology has something to do with the issue, although it is too often used as an excuse for sex discrimination. Of course, it is the wife who must bear the children, unless a couple adopts, and so the physical difficulties are exclusively hers. The physical demands presented by pregnancy, childbirth and breast feeding (if she chooses to do so) all place an added burden on the working mother or mother-to-be. This is especially true in the United States where the biological differences between men and women are most often taken as a justification for discrimination rather than an opportunity to protect legal rights.

Finally, women more often make the sacrifices to have children because that is what they have been brought up to do. A recent survey of 180 undergraduate women found that the majority of them would choose having a child over career advancement. The same would not be true of men. Women quickly face the fact that professional and management-level jobs, in particular, demand too much to be easily combined with motherhood. That may be a major reason why few women seek such occupations.

Joan Beck reported in the *Chicago Tribune* that of eighty female valedictorians who graduated from Illinois high schools in 1981, a majority had scaled down their career aspirations six years after graduation. These women were perhaps choosing in advance to avoid the conflict between careers and children by simply avoiding careers that could prove to be too demanding. That is a sacrifice not of a present career but of an opportunity not grasped.[7]

What Happens When You Give Up a Career?

It was eighteen inches tall and was hand delivered to me by two giggly boys on Mother's Day. "You work hard and sacrifice a lot to raise your kids and what do you get?" the card said on the front. Inside, it continued, "a card filled with love and thanks."

"Is this what I get for sacrificing my career?" I thought. I appreciated the sentiment, but it raised a host of mixed emotions.

Did I sacrifice my career? I think I did, though it was only partly intentional. My husband and I had been married four years before we decided to have children. We were both active professionally, and I was naively convinced I did not have to give up my aspirations once kids came along.

Instead, I dropped down to part-time work, intending to return to full-time once both children were past infancy. We hired a dear older woman who loved our kids and showered them with lots of attention as their baby-sitter. I remember writing in one of our Christmas letters, "God gives the resources needed to do that which He wants us to do."

I fully believed that, and I still do. But events at work took an unexpected turn, much of it related to the fact that I was a part-time worker. Ironically, I ended up leaving my career when my oldest child was already in school. I hoped to pick up another job in a related field. But when I received that notable Mother's Day card, two years had passed since I'd left my job, and I was still undecided about professional direction. Our well-laid plans were not to be.

Many women of the baby-boom generation, like me, have put off childbearing in favor of careers. But sooner or later they have to face the fact that their time for bearing children is limited. That's when the difficult decision making begins.

As a woman passes thirty, her ability to conceive and to carry a baby to term begins to diminish. And the chance of having a child with a major congenital abnormality such as Down's Syndrome increases. So, as baby-boom women have entered their thirties many of them have put aside career aspirations in order to have children. Some of these women have returned to work on a part-time basis. Some have returned full-time, and some have not returned to work at all.

The women who do not return to work face some major adjustments, including a loss of income and self-esteem. We would like to look at some of those issues here in the process of helping women gather information to make their own decisions about children or career.

Loss of Self-Esteem

"What are you doing now? Are you still teaching at the university?" an ex-colleague asked me when I bumped into him unexpectedly one day.

"No, I'm not. I quit almost four years ago," I said.

"Oh, are you keeping active then doing research?"

"No, the last article I published was two years ago. I really am not doing much professionally now," I responded.

"I'm sorry to hear that. I thought you were still . . ."

"Don't be sorry. I'm very happy and much at peace with myself at this point in my life," I interrupted.

Dave was being genuinely friendly, but I did not want to be pitied. Indeed, I was no longer sensing the loss of my career at that time, certainly not as keenly as when I first quit. And although I had quit my job, I had become involved in many activities which interested me, such as the local school board committees, church work, my husband's business and my three boys' many interests.

The most difficult thing to handle after ending an active career is the loss of self-esteem that came from knowing that you performed a needed function in the workplace. When you no longer have a title, when you can't answer the question, "what do you do?" you have lost something that was an important part of your identity. This is especially true if you had prepared a long time for your career or if you particularly enjoyed your work.

Should You Be the Working Mom?

Both Jason and Susan were practicing physicians until their first child became autistic. Randy is now fourteen years old and still cannot speak. Susan never returned to work and will probably never be able to get the retraining she would need to renew her license. Jason and Susan love Randy and his other, normal, siblings. But the sense of loss over Susan's career hangs onto them. She gave up a hard-earned skill and qualification.

"I have lost a large part of my identity," she told me. "I had worked towards my medical degree since I was twelve years old, but now that my oldest, normal child is 12, he doesn't even know that his mom is a medical doctor. He can't even be proud of me that way."

This sense of loss over a career does not mean that a mother doesn't appreciate her parenting role. It just means that one role has been lost in favor of another.

When you have been involved in a particular job or field of endeavor for a time, you become absorbed into the peculiar values and ways of thinking of that field. And some values make it particularly difficult to adapt to the new role of motherhood.

For example, I was involved in college teaching. People in the academic world value research, publishing, and professional advancement. There is a certain snobbery toward non-academic occupations. Like most folk in that world, I could not immediately shed those values when leaving that world. Even though I left voluntarily, I was still sensitive to the fact that I was no longer doing research, writing, or training others in an academic career. I still held those values even though I could not live up to them.

When a woman grows up in a home which values outside involvement and professionalism, she will also have trouble adjusting to being "just a homemaker." She has been taught since birth—or at least since entering college—that her worth depended in some sense on what she was doing.

In 1986 the Harvard-Radcliffe Christian Fellowship published a magazine in celebration of the 350th anniversary of Harvard University. The magazine carried an article by a full-time mother who had graduated from Radcliffe College. She told of a time when the alumni office sent a questionnaire to find out what alumni were doing. To her great relief, in the column of choices she found one called "child-raising interlude" and quickly marked it. Whoever designed the questionnaire was unusually sensitive to the fact that those who were spending their time at home might find it a put-down to answer "nothing" or "other" to that question.

Loss of Income

Of course, raising children is far from doing "nothing," but it doesn't count as a paid occupation. That's where another big adjustment to giving up a career comes in. Besides losing the self-esteem associated with paid employment, you also lose the income. You may end up on a very tight family budget just at a time when you would rather not deal with money problems. It's best to be prepared for this and to involve as many family members as possible in the decisions needed to decrease spending.

The one-income family tends to have more time (at least Mom does) but less money, so you can look for ways to save money that you would not have tried before because they were too time-consuming. For example, perhaps you might enjoy growing your own vegetables. That's time-consuming, but it's something that children can help with, and you might find it a way of spending quality time together.

Instead of taking family vacations in airplanes and hotels, you can try camping together. Again, it's a very different experience, but one the children might particularly appreciate. Table games like Clue or Monopoly can replace going to the movies. Do you like Chinese food? Try your hand at cooking it instead of eating out. Any kind of fancier cooking or baking might provide a sense of accomplishment. Now you have more time for those things, and doing your own cooking is cheaper than opening a frozen gourmet entree.

However, expect some resistance from the kids. While you as mother are trying to adjust to your loss of a career, they may have a hard time with the loss of income. While enjoying having you around more, they may not understand why you can't take a trip to Disney World or buy a new VCR like the neighbors have. That's why including them in the decision-making process (if they are old enough) is important. They have to be made to understand that having Mom around to go to ball games and to talk to after school has effects on other aspects of their lives.

Melinda stopped working when she discovered that her two teenagers were not getting along with each other in the hours after school before Mom got home. The girls had trouble disciplining themselves, and they needed someone to talk to in the afternoons. One of them was also having trouble in school.

Melinda enjoyed her job and had a sense of accomplishment from it, but she felt the kids needed her more. Since she has been home they have settled down, begun relating better to each other, and begun enjoying activities with Mom. But now they complain because they can't buy the extra car the family had talked about before Melinda quit! "You feel guilty no matter whether you work or don't!" Melinda said. Fortunately, she got over those feelings quickly. She recognized that the children could and should learn to live with compromises. "You just can't have everything your way!" she said, and she stopped feeling guilty that her family couldn't either.

Loss of Family Honor

There's something else that can happen when a mother quits her job. All of a sudden everyone in the family raises their expectations of what Mom can do for them.

However, just because you're not working outside the home, you don't need to take on the role of doormat. You still have a right to privacy, time for yourself, and creative outlets. You need to make sure that your family respects your need for continued personal growth and challenge. You risk becoming resentful of your family if you don't provide for your own needs.

For example, you have a right to personal friendships. If most of those were related to your work, then you need to make a special effort to find friends elsewhere. Perhaps there are mothers in your neighborhood that you might enjoy. You could form a play group—letting your kids play together while you spend time with each other.

If you have infants or toddlers at home, you might want to try to budget for a sitter or a preschool a couple of mornings a week so that you can have time for activities that you enjoy. Otherwise, talk to your husband about when he might be able to watch the kids—perhaps an evening each week—so that you can get away.

Even though you are not working outside the home, you and your husband should not assume that all the household chores should now be yours. Most persons—male or female—don't enjoy doing drudgery like cleaning the oven or washing the floors. Those sorts of tasks should still be shared if at all possible.

Studies show that the degree of authority between husbands and wives—and perhaps we could add the degree of respect—is affected by their relative incomes. Just as a working woman who quits her job loses self-esteem because she no longer produces an income—an important aspect of personhood in a money-based society—so she can also lose the respect of her husband.

Therefore, Dad has to remember that Mom is providing valuable services at home doing things which otherwise would cost a lot to have done. Like any other valued worker, Mom needs time off and vacations from her work. And she needs the help and honor of everyone in the family, not just on Mother's Day but all year.

Boredom and Joy

The final negative consequence of quitting a job is boredom. Even though few women want to admit it, taking care of children day in and day out can be simply boring, especially if you had a challenging career before. If you're the kind of person who loves to cook, clean, do home crafts, read the same book aloud five times per day, play kid games, or talk on the phone, then you may easily make the switch to staying home. But if your interests tend to lie along nondomestic lines, you'll face boredom when you stay home full-time.

Spending your time wisely takes a good deal of discipline. It takes discipline, for instance, for some women to forego the temptations of daytime TV. One church elder's wife confessed that she had an ongoing battle to keep the soap operas off during the day when her children were in school. She had to fill her time with other productive activities.

When Miriam quit her receptionist's job to be available when her kids came home from school, she also had a struggle to fill boring daytime hours. Of course, there were plenty of chores to do around the house, and it helped to be able to do those before the family returned from school and work. But that didn't satisfy her other interests. So she began voluntarily cleaning house for an elderly lady from her church and found that she enjoyed the friendship that developed with the woman. She also started a neighborhood Bible study group.

Friends of hers are active in the local PTA and volunteer at hospitals, nursing homes, and rescue missions. Some are politically active as well. They've found a sense of enjoyment in doing things that they didn't have time for before.

So, while it's true that women who give up careers have a big adjustment to make, they also have a lot of opportunities for pleasure. Working parents necessarily miss out on some special moments shared with their kids. You can't plan those special experiences into a busy day. They tend to happen spontaneously, often when you least expect them.

I was in my bedroom once picking up some clothes when

my four year old came running in and began jumping up and down.

"You seem very happy today," I said.

"Yes, I am," replied Paul.

"Well, I'm glad you're happy. Tell me why," I said.

"I'm happy because you are here!" His statement was a special gift to a mom at home.

"People ask me if I regret missing out on things Tricia does for the first time," said Susan. She returned to law school full-time after her daughter's first birthday. "I say no because even though she may speak her first sentence to a sitter, I still have the chance to hear the first sentence she says to me." Working parents have to learn not to oversentimentalize the little achievements which they may miss. But it's also true that they simply don't have as much time to spend with their children as at-home parents do.

Your kids are yours—no one else's. Seeing them grow up is an incomparable experience. Even though losing a career is a major loss, so is losing out on a childhood. That's the biggest compensation there is to the mother who sacrifices a job for her children. She has the special reward of being there for her kids at all the important times of their lives.

Alternatives

We've looked in this chapter at the trade-offs that most parents must make these days. Some choose to forego having children while others choose to sacrifice paid employment. Either way there is a sense of loss. But some mothers are lucky enough to be able to combine some sort of part-time career with raising children, or at least to give up their careers gradually.

Some twenty years ago Ginger was a married woman and full-time teacher. She thoroughly enjoyed her work in an era when women had yet to make their numbers felt in the marketplace. When her first child came along she cut down to part-time work in the extracurricular teaching areas. Then three years later twins arrived. She stopped working under contract but continued to substitute teach. She gradually taught less and less over the next few years until she finally quit altogether. But because she had made the change gradually, she did not face the usual grief that accompanies losing a career.

Some companies will allow employees to cut down to part-time work, perhaps even without loss of benefits. This is especially true if one works for smaller enterprises (which often have more flexibility) or if one has worked for the same company for several years. Some companies will even guarantee that the woman can return to full-time work when she desires, although that is still a rare guarantee. There aren't many guarantees for working mothers in America!

Other women have been able to arrange to work some hours at home. This minimizes the cost of child care and can allow a woman to continue working full-time while only leaving her children part-time. Computer technology has especially advanced the cause of these "home workers," although the laws and company policies have not caught up with this trend.

Finally, there are mothers who have skills that allow them to become self-employed. This is what Bette did. She worked full-time as a secretary for a few years after her marriage, but she also took in sewing on the side. Before children came along, she decided to quit her job and take in more sewing to do at home. Her business grew steadily, and she has continued to sew through the birth and raising of her two children. Her second child, Jenny, is now sixteen. Jenny said of her mom's situation, "It was great that she worked at home because she was always there when we needed her."

When you are self-employed, you set your own hours and conditions of work. Your family is more likely to find you "there" whenever you are needed. While not everyone has such a skill or opportunity, it is nevertheless something to look into as an alternative to quitting work altogether.

Having Your Cake and Eating It, Too?

Working mothers are often accused of trying to have their cake and eat it, too. This attitude implies that women do not have a right to both a career and children. However, there is no law that says men have this right but women don't. It is only tradition.

Society makes it very difficult for women to enjoy both career and motherhood fully. The typical working mother has compromised too much in both career and family life to feel that she's eating cake. Mothers who work because they must in order to provide for their families, mothers who are committed to careers without being any less committed to their families, and mothers who work out of a sense of calling—these mothers are far from trying to have it all.

"We've had our tears," said Lisa, the doctor whose son was born halfway through her medical training. "But what has seen Jon and me through is our very strong sense of calling."

Combining motherhood and a career requires a lot of sacrifice but it is not impossible. And children growing up in this situation can turn out right. One couple, the Travises, both worked throughout their child-raising years. Now their two girls are grown and have graduated from seminary. Another such couple is the Chungs. Their three children were closely spaced and at one point were all in college together. Their two eldest are now in medical school while the third is spending a few months as a volunteer with a Christian relief organization overseas.

Will you try to have children and a career, or will you choose between them? Either way, the choice is a sobering one. We will look at the options further in the chapters to come.

4

IS MONEY A REASON TO WORK?

JUST AFTER TOM AND JANE WERE MARRIED, THEY BOUGHT a life insurance policy on Tom. Even though Jane also worked, they felt that Tom's income was all they needed to pay the bills. They used the usual insurance-company formula for deciding how much insurance to buy and figured into it their plans to have two children.

They felt that they had bought plenty of insurance for a number of years to come. But, to their surprise, each year their insurance salesman called again to check on them. Had their income risen? If so, didn't they think they needed more insurance?

At first their answer was always an adamant no. They felt that their increase in income was not an appropriate reason for adding insurance. They could always live again on what they had been making. And the increased income had allowed them to save more. So they might actually need less insurance, they reasoned.

However, the insurance agent's persistence eventually paid off. Tom and Jane had to agree that their needs had increased with their income. They had moved to a larger home and had higher mortgage payments to make along with a new car loan. They wanted to send the kids to private school and to visit Grandma and Grandpa, who were out of state, regularly. All that would require extra money.

Tom and Jane are typical of most of us. Though they live

better than they did several years ago, they do not consider their life-style lavish. But they had to recognize that their expenses had indeed grown with their income. Just as work tends to expand to fill available time, so *Life-styles tend to rise along with incomes*. Yet we only become conscious of the change in life-style if we are forced to return to a lower income level.

How Much Is Enough?

Most mothers who work do so for the money, according to various statistics. Are these women sacrificing their families on an altar of materialism? Or are they working to give their kids the best? Is it wrong for a mother to work for the sake of money if her family is not in dire financial need? What is financial necessity? These are some of the issues we'd like to examine in this chapter.

A radio talk show one day featured a marriage and family counselor. He told of a couple who came to him to discuss their marriage problems. "We don't have enough money and it's causing friction," they said. The counselor asked them how much they made. They told him that without the wife's income they would have only sixteen thousand dollars per year, so the wife also worked. The counselor could well see why.

The next week another couple came to see him. They also traced their marriage difficulties to money. How much did they make? Thirty-two thousand dollars.

A third couple also felt that extra income would relieve the stress on their marriage. They made forty-eight thousand dollars per year.

The counselor made his point. We all have a tendency to either want more or to think that a little extra money will solve our problems. This is due largely to the fact that in our society many of our "needs" are man-made, created by an economy that thrives on arousing new consumer desires.

So, before trying to decide if a second paycheck is essential, we should look at our life-styles. We should check out our expenditures to see if it wouldn't be possible to decrease our spending to match one income. Many people feel trapped by the need for two incomes when in fact they could live on one if they were willing to adjust their needs to match. Do you need the motorbike? Could you eat out less each month? Would your kids survive in the YMCA pool rather than taking private swimming lessons?

Here's a handy, though not scientifically designed chart to determine the approximate level of your life-style. Answer the questions and then read the instructions at the end for totalling your answers.

1. How many records or tapes have you bought in the last six months?
   a. none (0)
   b. 1-2 (1)
   c. 3-4 (2)
   d. 5 or more (3)
2. Do you heat your home to 70 degrees or more on winter days?
   a. no (0)
   b. yes (2)
3. Has soda pop become a regular part of your diet?
   a. no (0)
   b. yes (2)
4. Has your child taken (or would you want him or her to take) swimming lessons before age three?
   a. no (0)
   b. maybe (1)
   c. yes (2)
5. Do you buy pancake mix or frozen pancake fixings?
   a. don't eat pancakes or make from scratch (0)
   b. buy pancake mix (1)
   c. buy frozen pancakes or frozen batter (2)
6. How often do you and your spouse go out to eat at a sit-down restaurant?

a. about 3 times/year (0)
b. about 4-6 times/year (1)
c. almost once a month or more often (2)

7. How often do you take the children to a fast-food or similar restaurant?
   a. 0-2 times/year (0)
   b. 4-6 times/year (1)
   c. about once a month or more often (2)
8. How often do you buy the most expensive cuts of beef such as prime rib or filet mignon?
   a. once or twice a month (4)
   b. once every two or three months (2)
   c. once or twice per year (0)
9. Over the last 18 months, how many times have you or your family stayed in a hotel/motel/resort when it was not a business trip?
   a. two or more times (4)
   b. once (2)
   c. none (0)
10. How old was the last car you had before you traded to a newer one?
    a. more than six years (0)
    b. three to six years (2)
    c. less than three years (4)

Go back and add up all your scores using the numbers in parentheses. A score of 18 or more means you live (pardon us!) rather expensively. A score of 10 or less puts you in the modest range. Those scoring 11-17 are in the middle.

This rough gauge tells you two things. It gives you some idea of how expensive your present life-style is. And it offers you some sense of how much "fat" there is in your budget that could be trimmed if you would rather not rely on two incomes.

If you want to cut down on your life-style, then you can look at the sorts of items that have been mentioned here. List on four or five pages the items on which you spend money each month (don't just give general categories, like "food," but list individual food items). Then go through the list and ask about each item, "Could we do without this or substitute something less expensive?"

Be realistic. An unrealistic budget only leads to frustration and deficits. Add up the savings, and you will have a rough idea of how much less you could live on if you so chose. (Don't forget to include contributions to churches and charities and money to pay one-time or annual bills like insurance or car repairs.) Also, realize that there are monetary costs associated with a second income. If Mom goes to work, she will need to spend more on clothes, commuting, convenience items and child care.

Moderation

Most of us could use more discipline in our spending habits. We tend not to make and keep budgets. We don't save or give away as much as we should. We waste money on things that turn out to be of low quality or questionable use. (How many fad toys would fall into that category of things purchased because they were absolutely "essential" and then virtually neglected within just a few weeks' time?)

Yet on the other hand we don't want to spend our lives counting pennies. Just as many Christians fall victim to materialism, a few go to the other extreme of losing out on some of the joy of life because they are so hung up on how they spend their money. Either way, money can run your life.

God has put us on this earth in part to enjoy His creation. "God . . . richly provides us with everything for our enjoyment" (1 Tim. 6:17), Paul writes. And Jesus asked, "Which of you, if his son asks for bread, will give him a stone?" (Mt. 7:9). Money and life-style are issues which raise a lot of tough questions. The answers are not black and white. Is it wrong for a mother to work so her family can move to a bigger house or a better school? Is it okay for her to work to send the kids to a Christian school? Where should the lines be drawn?

I knew a college student who had a lot of regrets about his frugal upbringing. Barry was Chinese. His parents were middle-class, naturalized American citizens. They lived in an ethnically mixed, middle-class suburb.

One thing Barry remembers from childhood is the fact that he didn't wear the same kinds of designer jeans his friends wore. His classmates wore Levis, Lees, and other famous labels while Barry wore generic brands that sometimes didn't even fit well. He always felt a little out of place because he never seemed to look as sharp as his friends.

I could understand why Barry's parents didn't want to pay the exorbitant prices that many of the major brands commanded for their jeans. But I wondered if they ever realized the impact this had on Barry during the critical teen years when fitting in and being accepted were so important.

Except for not making money our god, it seems there are no absolute laws when it comes to things like financial values. Thrift and saving are good, but so is being sensitive to our children's needs (Eph. 6:4).

With this sensitivity in mind and with a desire to show affection in a tangible way, last spring I bought my nine-year-old son a Chicago Cubs jacket. It cost some ten dollars more than one without the Cubs name, but it was worth it. He wore it to school the very next day and every day after that, even though the temperature swung between thirty-five degrees and seventy!

Making Values Practical

It is difficult to tread the fine line between laying up treasures in Heaven instead of on earth and giving our families good things. How do we strike a consistent balance?

It might help to sit down with your spouse and make a prioritized list of your values. Is travel more important to you than fancy home appliances? Or would you rather stay at home but be very comfortable while you're there? Is it more important to you to save for your child's education or give that child all the best while she's growing up? Try to determine what goals are most important to you and your family. Then test out your priorities when it comes to making financial decisions. Revise the list if it seems clear that what you're actually doing doesn't match. Or revise your expenditures if they don't match your determined goals.

The purpose of all this is to help you determine if you really need two incomes or not. If you can meet your goals on one income without too much friction or discomfort, then money is not a reason for both parents to work. But if your goals are not being met, and if you're convinced the goals shouldn't be revised, then both Mom and Dad will probably have to work. No one can decide for you whether you need two incomes. There's no absolute income level above which it becomes sinful for a mother to work. It all depends on life-styles and values, which ought to be biblically informed but can't be absolutely determined.

If your children are old enough, you should try to involve them in the question of whether Mom should work for financial reasons. To teenagers one might say, "Mom and Dad think we should try to get a larger home so that you can each have a room of your own. Is that important to you? It would mean that Mom has to go to work and would not be as available as she is now. You would have to pack your own lunch in the morning, take on two extra chores each around the house, and be more consistent about cleaning your room. We also won't have as many fancy meals and home-baked loaves of bread as we do now, unless you want to do the cooking. How would you feel about such changes? Is it worth it to you to have your own rooms?"

Of course, a younger child can't be expected to make such a difficult decision. But you might say this to an eight year old: "You sure like going to spend weekends with Grandma and Grandpa. Is it because you have a room there all to yourself? How would you feel if Mommy went to work so that we could save enough money to buy a house that would have a bedroom for each of you? That would mean that some evenings Daddy would give you dinner and put you to bed because Mommy would be working. Would that upset you?"

A lot of your child's response will be determined by the kinds of values he or she has already developed in your home. Like you, a child's wants and needs will tend to increase as the money available increases. It might take a conscious and concerted effort for your child to accept less in order to have Mommy around more.

When my youngest child, Paul, was three I took him to the travel agent to pick up tickets for our family's trip to Colorado. Paul had no idea what an airplane trip would be like. But when the travel agent handed over the tickets, explaining that they would allow us to board the plane, Paul surprised us both. A huge smile broke across his face, and he jumped for joy. "Boy, Paul," said the agent, "you really make my job worthwhile."

Less than a year later we again took a plane trip together. Soon afterward Paul came to me and emphatically declared, "It's not fair! I never get to go to Disneyland, never!" His friend had just returned from Disneyland, and Paul had decided that such a trip was an essential element in his happiness.

In our society, it will take work to teach children to be content with what they have—which is probably far more than the average child of the world. One thing we can do is to give them information about how the rest of the world lives. Last year I brought home a brochure from a Christian relief and development organization. Each day prior to Thanksgiving we read one story out of the brochure. Each story outlined one type of situation of suffering—poverty, hunger, refugees, etc. Jason, our seven year old, decided to contribute two dollars to buy a pig for a needy family. But then Stephen, the nine year old, thought they should split the cost of the eighteen-dollar pig. So he gave nine dollars from his savings and Jason came up with another seven. Then Paul dumped out his piggy bank and contributed the change.

A second way that children can come to view themselves as fortunate rather than deprived is for us to teach them to be thankful for the things that they are able to enjoy. Saying thanks is not only polite—it also recognizes that you do not necessarily have a right to what you get. It prevents taking a privilege for granted.

Since our oldest son, Stephen, was five, he has always enjoyed eating out. When he turned nine, he began to be choosy about food. When we were on vacation recently, we ate out several times. Each time, he would choose a shrimp dish. After the third time, I took him aside and said, "Stephen, you know that shrimp is very expensive. I don't want you to think that you have a right to order it every time we are in a restaurant. Eating out is itself a treat." I also told him of a family he knows personally but did not realize they could not afford to eat out. The next time we were in a restaurant, I was glad to see that he ordered a chiliburger instead of shrimp.

A third thing we can do is to give our children practical experience with money. Our boys are given the opportunity to buy some of the things they want, even though there's no store within walking distance of our home. We don't like to spend a lot of family money on sweets, gum, and soda pop. But we stock those things in a family "store" so the boys can buy them with their allowance money. We are waiting to see if they will decide that pop or gum is not worth the cost to enjoy it.

How Much for That Baby?

It's one thing, of course, to talk about money values with children. It's another to determine how much it costs to have a child in the first place. In recent years we have seen trends toward having smaller families, not having children at all, or postponing childbearing until later in life. All these trends are at least indirectly related to the cost of having children these days. In one study 60 percent of the mothers interviewed said that they did not want any more children because of the cost. The next most common reason—physical, emotional or age-related problems—drew only 11 percent of the vote. Apparently most mothers considered the cost of child rearing to be high.

So what are the costs? The greatest cost is an indirect one—the cost of losing a portion or all of the mother's income if she is working. Even mothers who intend to return to work full-time after childbirth often end up not doing so. They may enjoy motherhood so much that they decide to stay home. Or they may take longer maternity leaves or return to work only part-time.

The indirect cost of the child, then, depends on how much the mother makes and how much of her income is lost. If she stays at home until her children start school, and if she has more than one child, then she may lose seven, eight, nine or more years of income. If she returns to work shortly after her child is born then she loses less income. If she reduces her work to part-time, she reduces her income proportionately.

Women who take time off to have children also lose out on the raises and promotions that they might have received if they had continued working without a pause or had continued working full-time. Economist Sylvia Ann Hewlett estimates that "If a woman takes time off to have a child and get it through preschool, her future earnings are 13 to 19 per cent lower for the rest of her life."[1]

A woman in a career-oriented position who chooses to reduce her hours to part-time must face the fact that this may reduce her income by more than just the reduction of hours. She will probably be ineligible for various promotions by opting into part-time work. I found this out the hard way. When I had taught enough years to qualify for a promotion, I was no longer eligible because I was working part-time. That rule was later changed, but too late to benefit me.

All these factors have to be taken into consideration if one is seriously trying to put a monetary cost on having a child. A couple who are enjoying two paychecks now but plan to have children should take care not to get used to living so expensively that the loss of one of those paychecks will be a difficult adjustment. It would be well to lay aside more of that extra income now for the future.

Direct Costs

When children are added to a family, there will certainly be additional expenses—the direct cost of feeding, clothing, housing, educating, and entertaining a child. Those are the costs that most often drive women back to work even if they want to stay home.

The U.S. Department of Agriculture has estimated that the cost of raising a child born in 1979 to age seventeen was about $134,400. That includes $41,000 for housing, $33,000 for food and $20,000 for transportation.

In another study by Thomas Espenshade, the cost of raising a child to age 22 (thus including a college education) was $85,000 in 1980 dollars, assuming a *modest* standard of living and attendance at a state university.[2] But many researchers consider this much too low.

Lawrence Olson estimated that an average American family could expect to spend $226,000 to raise a firstborn son to age 22 and $247,000 to raise a firstborn daughter to that age (in 1982 dollars).[3] What a difference!

Olson's estimates are so much higher in part because he is looking only at firstborns. Subsequent children are much less expensive to raise because many costs do not have to be repeated—such as the cost of baby equipment, housing space, utilities, medical insurance, and some clothing. Depending on spacing, the cost of a second child may be half that of the first.

Second, Olson was assuming a much less "modest" standard of living than Espenshade. He estimated that a low-income family would spend $121,000 for a firstborn son while high-income families might spend as much as $323,000.

That's value systems at work again! Income affects spending, and so the higher-income folk will spend more on their kids.

Our point is that much of what people spend on their children is under their own control. They can spend a lot or make do with little. And that's where your big decision comes in. Chances are yours is not a clear-cut case of absolute financial need. If you are like most parents today, you could easily make use of more money, but you could also survive on less. Which you do is pretty much up to you, the choices you make, and the values you share with your children.

Priorities and Choices

For many parents Mom's income is not necessary to put food on the table. But it may be essential when it comes to things like the down payment for a house, a new car or summer camp for the children. These parents have to set their own priorities. Is it more important to send the kids to camp or to spend more time with them each day?

Parents who work have less time for their children. That's true of mothers and fathers, too. Fathers need to build closer relationships with their kids. It may make more sense, then, for a mother to go to work if in so doing her husband can avoid having to take on a second job or working longer hours. That might allow them both to share more in the joys of parenthood, in providing for the children and in nurturing them.

In *Working and Caring,* Dr. T. Berry Brazelton suggests that some men may avoid developing a close bond with their infants out of an unconscious fear that their role as provider may be made more difficult—leaving home in the morning may be harder if you enjoy the new baby. Some fathers secretly envy the time their wives have to spend with their children. If some women feel locked into their societal roles as full-time mothers, some fathers also feel constrained by the role our culture demands they play.[4]

Men who are sole breadwinners may feel trapped in their

jobs. Having a working wife might free them up to explore their options a bit more, to try a different field or even to set up their own business.

Should Mom work? The answer usually boils down to this—setting priorities and making choices. Living in America there are few things about which we do not have a choice, unless we give up our freedom to explore new possibilities and options. As people made in God's image with freedom of will, we have many choices to make in life. One of these is whether to marry and have children. Another is whether to work after children are born. The more aware we become of how our lives are interconnected—income, life-style, number of children—the more capable we will be of exercising control over our circumstances rather than being controlled by them.

5

WHAT HAPPENS TO YOUR KIDS?

Given the breakdown of family life in Western countries—with rampant divorce, single parents, working mothers, absentee fathers, etc.—it is only fitting that . . . churches are placing fresh emphasis on God's design for the home."

That's what the director of a respected missions organization said recently in his mission's magazine. In his eyes working mothers are right up there with divorce and absentee fathers. Is that what working motherhood is all about? Are working mothers hurting their kids and ruining their families?

When *Redbook* magazine polled their readers in 1986, 75 percent of at-home mothers and 50 percent of working mothers agreed with the statement that a working mother's children almost always suffer. The same poll showed, however, that 68 percent of working mothers and 42 percent of at-home mothers believed that the children would not suffer if they had good substitute care.[1]

Newsweek magazine received more positive results in its poll. When asked, "Do you think a mother who works . . . can adequately fulfill her responsibilities to her child?" 50 percent of the women answered yes if the mother worked full-time and 86 percent answered yes if she worked part-time.[2] But again, although working mothers were much more prone to answer yes to such questions, a surprisingly large portion of them still responded negatively. That fact reflects the ambivalence with which mothers approach work. Even those who choose to combine motherhood and work see the many problems which come from trying to juggle priorities, finding good substitute care, and trying to fulfill an ideal image of what every mother should be. And the biggest question facing every mother considering work is, how will it affect my children?

What the Children Think

Although it may not yield scientific data, it always helps to ask your children what they think about having working parents. It can be reassuring to talk to them years later, too.

Pat had just received her nursing certification when she married Jeff. Their first child came along quickly and unplanned, so she decided to continue working because she wanted to use her hard-earned credentials. She truly loved her work and determined to grin and bear the criticisms she received from family members and friends. After their second child was born she cut down to part-time, and then switched to occasional, on-call work when twins arrived three years later. Meanwhile, her paycheck enabled Jeff to take the risk of leaving his job to pursue a new career. Today he is a successful insurance agent.

Their children range in age from twenty-four to sixteen. Pat talked to her two oldest kids about what it was like to have a working mother. "I felt guilty sometimes when I had to wake Dick and Jan up early to take them to the baby-sitter's," Pat said about her experience as a working mother. Nevertheless, the children don't seem to have minded.

Asked if he ever wished his mom didn't work, Dick replied, "No. I had a blast!" The baby-sitter had a boy a year older than Dick, and the two became close playmates. Dick looks back on those years as happy—even happier than they would have been if he had stayed at home with his mom and younger sister all the time. Dick's sister, Jan, was also positive about her mother's working.

Usually if a child is suffering daily because of a parent's work, there will be evidence of the problem. Most children are open and honest. If they are having a consistently bad experience with a baby-sitter or day-care center, they will show it by continually balking when it's time to go (of course, occasional balking is to be expected!).

But most parents aren't so concerned about the immediate effects of a particular day-care situation as about the long-term, unnoticeable (at the time) but detrimental effects of a mother's job. Behind the statement "a child needs its mother" is the common belief that no one but Mother will do, and that if a child does not have its mother available to him most of the time some deep psychological harm will result. That's what working mothers fear. Is this fear well-founded?

Infants and Toddlers

Of course, all experts agree that infants need to form a close emotional bond with at least one person. In most cases this is the natural parents, unless they have given up custody to an adoptive parent or guardian.

Studies of infants, such as orphans, raised in institutional settings, show retarded development. But these are extreme situations where the children are not talked to, played with or otherwise provided with human contact beyond the basic contact of feeding and cleaning. In normal circumstances, parents and children do not have to spend all their waking hours together in order to establish and maintain a solid, nurturing relationship.

Infants in most cases do establish a deep bond with their working mothers. This bond begins to grow at birth. Evidence now indicates that during the hours just after birth a baby is particularly alert and receptive to human interactions. Thus, most hospitals now allow parents to cuddle their newborns for a couple of hours after delivery. That's also one reason why anesthesia is now discouraged for labor and delivery. It interferes with both the mother's and infant's ability to bond.

This bonding continues during the days, weeks, and months to come. It is not clear just how long it takes nor when the process can be considered complete. A 1987 study showed that 54 percent of infants whose mothers worked full-time by the time they were eight months old formed secure attachments with their mothers. A much higher percentage—71 percent—of infants of at-home mothers formed secure attachments.[3]

Bonding is a difficult thing to measure. It also may differ from child to child and parent to parent. While an easy, happy baby may bond easily to its mother and vice versa, a difficult, cranky baby may take longer. At any rate, a mother may need extra time to bond to a difficult baby simply because of the ambivalent feelings which a tiresome infant raises.

Pediatrician T. Berry Brazelton in *Working and Caring* suggests that mothers put off returning to work until their babies are four months old.[1] This allows them to get beyond the demanding first three months and develop a happy relationship with each other. Then, says Brazelton, the best time for a mother to return to work is at a time when her baby is not learning a demanding new skill. Times to avoid returning to work are from seven to nine months when stranger anxiety is at a peak and the baby is learning to crawl, and from twelve to sixteen months when the child is mastering the skill of walking and has a heightened fear of separation from Mother. But these ages are approximate as each child develops at his own rate, and parents must take their cues from their own child.[4]

If the alternate care is consistent and attentive, it should not be harmful to a child. In fact, most experts believe it is good for a child to relate to someone other than Mother. That's one reason why most experts wish fathers would take a more active role in parenting. Fathers tend to interact with their children differently from mothers—in a more playful and stimulating manner. Children benefit from various kinds of stimulation.

Stability is the most critical factor in early child care. Thus, a steady baby-sitter is probably better for an infant or toddler than a day-care center because of the staff turnover in day-care centers.

Controversy over Day Care

In the 1970s and early 1980s, studies that were conducted on the effects of day care on the psychological development of children seemed to indicate that children could thrive in such situations if the day care is of consistently good quality. A 1973 study showed that children who began day care as babies were less tense and more sociable than those who began at age three or so. A 1985 study came up with similar findings.[2]

But controversy has recently arisen over the conclusion drawn from these studies that day care is not detrimental to child development. This disagreement is focused on children who began day care at eighteen months of age or less and who are in day care for more than 20 hours per week. Some experts, especially Jay Belsky of Pennsylvania State University, have found evidence to raise red flags.[5]

Belsky cites such studies as a 1982 one in which preschool personnel observed that children who had been in group day care since infancy seemed more anxious, aggressive and hyperactive. Another study was conducted in 1984. It looked at a group of 107 toddlers, some of whom had been in day care more than 20 hours per week and some who had not. Researchers found that 62 percent of the former group appeared to be insecure as compared to 31 percent of the latter. Jay Belsky believes that children who began day care before eighteen months of age present their parents with more behavioral problems when they reach the ages of nine or ten.

These disagreements among the experts leaves mothers with little consistent, clear information to help them make the crucial decision about substitute care for their infants and toddlers. However, the studies do seem to indicate that part-time care by a substitute care giver is better than full-time care. Further, infants and toddlers seem to do better with an attentive, warm, nurturing individual rather than a group-care situation. But little can be said beyond these basics. The verdict is not yet in on this issue.

One thing, however, is clear: Mothers need not fear that their children will form a closer bond to a baby-sitter than to themselves. The parent-child bond is too strong to be easily altered.

This fear and another, similar one that their children will forget them, are part of the issue that has not been studied very well—the effect of working on mothers. Many mothers report missing their young children tremendously when they return to work. There were many times when I should have been given a speeding ticket as I raced home after work to see my firstborn child. And I was especially miserable when I had to attend a conference out of town when my son was only seven months old. These feelings are natural, and mothers should expect them as they consider the consequences of working. It can be a very emotionally trying experience!

School-Age Children

Unlike preschoolers, school-age children do not need day care except for the time between the end of school and the end of the parents' workday. But there are still questions to be asked about the effect a mother's work has on her school-age children.

Several studies have focused on a possible link between delinquency and maternal employment. Three such studies found an association between a mother's working and delinquent behavior among middle-class youth but not lower-class youth.[6] This seems hard to explain. Why would social class have an influence on whether a mother's working affects a child's behavior? The answer is unclear. Probably, this just points out the complexity of human behavior.

In fact, some other studies found that it was not mother's working in itself that contributed to delinquency. Instead, what was important was whether the youngster was adequately supervised when at home.[7] A child's behavior stems from a number of factors, including the emotional environment at home, parental discipline, peer influence, the atmosphere at school and, of course, the child's free choices. One cannot blame bad behavior on a single factor like work.

Other studies have looked at working mothers and academic achievement. Four educators conducted a recent, five-year study covering 573 elementary school students in 38 states. They found that children of working mothers have higher IQ scores, lower absenteeism and better performance in reading and math than children of nonworking mothers. Children of working mothers also had better communication skills, were more involved in school activities, and were more capable of doing things for themselves. Thus, this study found favorable characteristics among the children of working mothers.[8]

A similar but older study, however, had mixed results, depending on the sex and socioeconomic class of the child. In the middle class, boys with working mothers had lower test scores than boys whose mothers were full-time homemakers. In lower classes, boys with working mothers did better in school and had higher educational aspirations than boys with nonworking moms. For girls, in all economic classes those with working mothers did better in school and had higher aspirations than those with nonworking moms.[9]

What does all that mean? Should middle-class mothers of boys stay home and mothers of girls go to work? What if you've got a son and a daughter! Again, the studies point out how difficult it is to draw from statistics alone any significant conclusions about the source of certain human behaviors. There are too many factors involved.

What is more important is that parents consider for themselves what effect their work might be having on their children. Both fathers and mothers need to be sure that their children are receiving the love, supervision, and discipline they need from both parents. They should pay attention to both how their children are doing in school and how they behave outside of school.

Generally, the consensus of researchers at this point seems to be that children of working mothers develop about as normally as other children. The crucial issue is not whether a mother works but how effective *both* parents are *as parents.* Anyone, whether working or not, can be a bad disciplinarian or an emotionally (or physically) abusive parent. And working mothers are about as capable as nonworking mothers of avoiding the pitfalls of bad parenting.

Differences Real or Imagined?

There are indeed differences between the children of working mothers and those of nonworking mothers. But those differences tend to be neutral (rather than negative) or temporary, not destructive and permanent. First, children of working mothers often enjoy a higher income. Financial stress is one common source of family problems. So Mom's working can help. In 1979, for instance, the proportion of families with both spouses present that had incomes below the poverty line was 3.8 percent. It would have been 14.8 percent without working wives.[10]

Terri's husband walked out on her over a year ago. They are now in the process of getting a divorce, and Terri is considering going back to work. She is trained as a dental assistant, but she quit working when the first of their three children was born eight years ago. If she does not go back to work now, she and the children will have to live on an extremely tight budget. That's what they're doing now, and Terri has noticed the difference having a little extra money can make.

"The other day," she said, "a friend gave me some money and told me to take the kids out to a fast-food restaurant to eat. I did, and we had such a good time." The little extras like that—going to a museum or the zoo, going to summer camp, eating out—are often the kinds of things that come out of a mother's extra income. In research interviews, children have expressed an appreciation of such extras. So should Mom work in order to provide such extras? That is a matter of setting priorities and making choices for your particular family.

The second demonstrated effect of having a working mother is housework. Children of working mothers do more housework. Is that bad? No. A reasonable level of household responsibilities that are appropriate for a child's age do him good rather than bad. As with putting on their jackets by themselves or tying their own shoelaces, helping around the house encourages independence and self-reliance in children. Many problems that arise among youth in this society result from their having too little sense of responsibility and no opportunity to feel useful. Children of working mothers may avoid this if they contribute their share to household needs.

Research indicates that children of working mothers have increased self-esteem, maturity, and sense of responsibility. "Working mothers seem to encourage independence more than mothers who don't work," Professor Lois Hoffman of the University of Michigan was quoted as saying in *Newsweek* magazine. "This is good for children . . . especially daughters. At-home mothers may do more for the child than is necessary." Expecting children to do what they can at each age level may also increase their drive to achieve in adult life.

Hoffman and other researchers have found that the daughters of working mothers seem to be more independent and outgoing, tend to be higher achievers, and have more respect for their mothers and women in general. Sons of working mothers also see women as more competent and, probably because of the higher involvement of fathers in their lives, see men as warmer than do boys whose mothers stay home.[11]

Finally, a third, clearly demonstrated effect of having a working mother is that Mother is not around as often. A working mom simply doesn't spend as much time in the same house with her children as her nonworking counterpart. But what that means for the kids depends largely on how it is handled by both Mom and Dad.

Research indicates that even mothers who stay home do not spend huge amounts of time in focused, individual attention with their children. They are in the same house with their kids, but they are busy doing chores. According to one study, the average at-home mother spends less than ten minutes per day playing with or reading to her preschool child. (Other researchers indicate that this can vary up to thirty minutes per day.) The same study found that working mothers spend as much time in direct interaction with their children as nonworking mothers.[12]

Where Happiness Lies

The biggest factor, as we've said before, in how children fare with their parents—working or at home—seems to be how happy the parents are with their choices of life-style. Mothers who work and feel good about it tend to do a better job than those who stay home but are frustrated. Likewise, mothers who stay home because they want to will often be better parents than those who work but hate their jobs.

Cathy was a high school economics teacher with three daughters aged nine through sixteen when she resigned her job. She was frustrated with the red tape and unsatisfactory working conditions. Five years later she had launched her own business as a travel agent. Her life was a whirlwind of travel, conventions, and business contacts.

We asked her daughters what they felt about their mother's work. "We think it's great," the oldest, who was in college then, replied. "She's very happy, and we're glad for that."

"The time when she didn't work," daughter number two chimed in, "was miserable. We would come home from school and find lists of things for each of us to do around the house. Because she had time on her hands and was restless 'not doing anything,' she tried to get everyone else to 'do something'!" Daughter number three nodded in agreement.

Three years later the oldest daughter had joined her mother's company and the other two were in college. Cathy's husband has his own business, too, and travels with Cathy whenever possible.

In a study by M. R. Yarrow and others, mothers were classified as homemakers or working mothers and as satisfied or dissatisfied. Then they were given scores on the adequacy of their mothering. Satisfied homemakers scored highest, while dissatisfied homemakers scored lowest. One reviewer said of this phenomenon, "Those women who stressed duty as the reason for being a full-time homemaker had the very lowest scores on mothering. One can speculate that the children of dissatisfied homemakers would be better off if their mothers were employed."[13]

Older children, in particular, often do not need or want Mom on their backs all the time. When I asked my ten-year-old son if children needed a full-time mother, he responded, "Kids need a little independence, you know." Was that a hint? Maternal attention can be too much of a good thing sometimes!

If full-time work cuts too deeply into time with the family, part-time work can be an ideal compromise if you can find such work that is interesting and stimulating. Research shows that adolescents with mothers who work part-time have better relationships with their parents than do those with non-working mothers.[14] And, while children of working mothers tend to do better in school than do those of at-home moms, children of mothers who worked part-time did the best of all.[15]

Whether parents succeed in providing their children with love, effective discipline and appropriate responsibility depends not so much on whether the mother works but on the emotional resources of the family. Is Mother happy? Is Dad? Is the marriage healthy? Or is there undue stress? When Mother and Dad are happy and satisfied with their roles, the family will get from them the attention and emotional responses it requires.

6

WHAT HAPPENS TO YOUR MARRIAGE?

Tom was a professor at a small college in Iowa. When his two children approached the teen years, his wife, Tina, resumed her teaching career in the public school. Within three years, Tina was tenured and making more than Tom. Tom began to fret about his job. He had a lot of responsibility and had single-handedly set up a certification program for students. But he was rewarded only with more responsibility, not more pay.

When an opportunity came up to switch to a better-paying job as the director of a center for disturbed teens, Tom did not hesitate. When asked why he changed positions after so many years, he said honestly, "It was the money. Not that we needed a higher income, but it bothered me that Tina was making more than me."

When a marriage is enlarged by the wife's going to work, changes begin to occur in the relationship. Some of these can create problems. Some can be used to strengthen the marriage. In this chapter we would like to examine several key changes that occur in marriages when the wife goes to work. Anyone considering taking that step should be aware of these changes and possible conflicts in order to better prepare for them.

Identity Crises

Ruth Jones and her daughter, Mindy, were visiting Ruth's

sister one day. As Mindy played "house" nearby, Ruth's sister asked her what she wanted to be when she grew up. Mindy replied, "I want to be just like Mommy. I want a blue house, and a baby girl just like my dolly."

At just six years of age, Mindy is beginning to carve out an identity for herself. She has learned that playing with dolls and playing house are appropriate games for girls. She wouldn't think of playing with trucks or work tools like her brother does. Those are "boy's games."

All of us grow up with ideas gained from our parents and our culture about what is appropriate behavior for the type of person we are. We turn these ideas into preferences and finally use these preferences to create our adult identities. When these chosen identities no longer fit the values that exist in our culture, then inner turmoil and conflict result.

In this book we've talked a lot about how men and women have grown up with particular views of what roles mothers and fathers should fulfill—fathers should be breadwinners and mothers should be homemakers. When mothers begin to work those roles are threatened, and the resulting identity crisis can cause difficulty for a marriage.

Tom felt threatened when his wife began to make more money than he did. Fortunately, he was able to change jobs and that solved the problem. But many men don't have that option and begin to feel trapped, taking out their frustrations on their wives as the source of their conflict. They have to work hard to reevaluate their role in the family and to learn to feel good about being the second-highest breadwinner. Their wives also must find ways to be sensitive to their needs for a changed self-image.

Wives can face similar difficulties. When Joe's wife, Vicki, began to work, Joe started pitching in eagerly with household duties. At first he made some bad, but understandable mistakes. When mending his son's pants, he jammed up the sewing machine. When washing the family's clothes, he ruined a blouse that should have been done by hand. But while Joe learned a lot and became able to do household tasks quite competently, Vicki was never able to accept that. She continued to criticize him and took the attitude that Joe could never do anything as well as she could. Finally, Joe stopped helping out except in emergencies.

Vicki explained her feelings: "Ever since I can remember my mom has prided herself on being a good homemaker. Once she even won a blue ribbon at the state fair for a pie she entered in a baking contest." Vicki had always wanted to be like her mom in the sense of being a good homemaker. So when Joe started helping out around the house she felt threatened by his actions. She felt it was an indictment of her ability to handle the housework and work outside, too. And when Joe became good at doing some things, she felt that her role as homemaker was threatened.

So long as husbands and wives act in ways that correspond to their sense of who they are, they feel good about themselves. But when their actions or those of others do not conform to that self-image, they begin to feel insecure. Oftentimes what our spouses do (Tom's wife making more money, Vicki's husband helping out at home) can make us feel threatened.

Spouses whose roles are changing like this will face tension in their marriages. They will have to give extra time to working through these tensions. But if they do that, they will find that their marriages and their own self-concepts can become better because of this testing.

Sharing Housework

When people get married, two contracts go into effect. One is the written, formal contract of the marriage license and vows. The other is an unwritten and unspoken contract—the informal but influential expectations that the spouses have of each other. These consist of the many assumptions that people have of what a husband or wife is supposed to be or do.

For example, a husband may assume that his job is to bring home a good paycheck while his wife is to watch over everything at home—cleaning the house, shopping for groceries, cooking, washing, caring for the kids, and remembering Aunt Mary and Uncle Harvey's anniversary. The wife might expect the husband to perform certain household chores such as emptying the trash, cutting the lawn and changing the oil in the car. If the husband doesn't do these things without being asked, then conflict results. The spouses are basing their expectations on how things worked in their parents' homes, not what they've discussed with their mates.

All these assumptions may be called into question when a wife begins to work. Typically, the woman will expect to get more help with the household tasks and child-rearing duties. But the husband still assumes she'll handle all that. And both may be reluctant to put their expectations into words.

In our study of one hundred suburban parents with school-aged children we found that slightly over four-fifths of non-working mothers assumed major responsibility for the care of the children. And this didn't change much when the mothers went to work. Two-thirds of working mothers also carried the major responsibility for child care.[1] While most of our respondents were Christians, other studies indicate that these figures hold true in the rest of the population. While the husbands of working mothers do seem to help more, the mothers still carry the major responsibility for all domestic tasks.

In addition to carrying the greater burden at home, working mothers also often shoulder an inordinate degree of responsibility at work. Because women still face prejudice in the workplace, especially in some occupations and at some levels, they may find that they must work harder just to stay even or to receive the same degree of acceptance as their male coworkers. These women are going to be particularly concerned that they get extra help at home.

However, a lot of men resist helping in this way. It's doing "women's work." Mary and Frank developed some critical problems in their marriage because they could not communicate about these issues. Mary went to work when their boys were five and nine years old. Without ever making her expectations clear, she began assuming Frank would help out around the house by shopping, doing the laundry or entertaining the kids. But Frank continued his previous life-style, reading the paper in the evenings.

Mary began dropping hints. She talked about another couple they knew where the husband baby-sat a lot and even washed diapers. Frank responded by saying that he "didn't have a flair" for such things. When conflicts developed between Mary's work and particular tasks (like going to a PTA meeting when she should be fixing dinner after work), she would again drop hints about needing help. But Frank either pretended not to hear or suggested compromises like "You can cook dinner when you get back from the meeting, and we can eat late."

Finally, Mary lost her cool and accused Frank of not caring enough to help out. That got her results, but not the ones she wanted. Frank started making excuses for not coming home at all. He would stay late at the office or stop to see friends on the way home. Now Mary is furious and doesn't know what to do. If they don't begin working on this problem soon the marriage may fall apart.

Communication is a critical link in any marriage. If a couple does not have a good basis for effective interaction before the wife goes to work, the conflicts that arise over household tasks can put extra pressure on the relationship. Mary's working did not *cause* the problems with Frank. Those bad habits of not talking directly about needs (her dropping hints and his ignoring them) were established long before she went to work. But the extra tension from her working brought the problems quickly to a crisis.

If one spouse carries an excessive amount of the household burden while both work, resentment is bound to build. However, the change brought about by a wife's working can be an occasion for establishing better habits of communication and for beginning to share parenting responsibilities. A stronger marriage *can* result, but only if the partners work hard at it.

Building Common Values

When a woman stays home with her children, her experiences and values are largely shaped by her tasks at home while her husband's experiences are shaped by his work environment. Then, when a woman goes to work, she begins to have work experiences of her own. In some marriages this change in perspective can cause conflict, in others it has a positive effect.

Some husbands find that when their wives begin to work the two of them begin to share more. They become closer companions because they can better understand how the other spends the workday. One husband, who was not threatened by this change, describes the experience:

> I had to learn . . . how not to be mad at someone who no longer pretended that I was the center of the universe. . . . As my wife's expertise in business deepened, it began to pay some surprising dividends. I could talk with her about how to get something done. I could ask her advice about difficult and complicated business problems. . . .
>
> We became more friendly as we became more involved with the same kinds of things. She no longer humored me; but she helped me. And that turns out to be a great relief.[2]

Further, just as working wives begin to understand the trials and triumphs of the marketplace, so (if they get more involved at home) their husbands can begin to better understand the frustrations and victories of running a household.

However, just as these new roles can enhance a marriage, they can also jeopardize it. The wife and the husband may drift farther apart if one of them adopts a new perspective that is different from the other's.

Ann first met Jim while she was earning her way through

college as a coffee shop hostess. After they got married, Jim kept his job as bank courier but Ann dropped out of school. At the birth of their first child she also quit her job. Another child came along soon. Six years later, one of Ann's former professors heard that she might be interested in a job and hired her as a chemistry lab technician.

In time, Ann's former ambitions to finish college returned. Under the influence of her professor and fellow chemistry majors, Ann is thinking of going into chemical research. However, Ann's talk about this career makes little sense to Jim. He has begun to suspect that Ann's professor has got her thinking she's better than she really is.

Ann feels distant from Jim. "Sometimes I think Jim and I live in two different worlds." Now he is pressing her to have another child.

Again, work and marriage can cause problems or resolve them. Much of it depends on how the couple handles the issues that arise, how secure the spouses are in their identities, and how strong their marriage was before the change took place.

Money

The old saying goes, "He who pays the piper calls the tune." In our society that is usually true. Money talks. It carries power. Even in families, authority tends to follow income.

A supermarket butcher remembers his childhood:

> While growing up I recall many a time when Mom would go out of her way to give Dad the best slice of meat. He was the first one to be served and, according to my mother, this was only proper. "After all," she would say, "Dad is our provider." In a way I guess you'd say that my dad was the C.E.O. and the V.I.P. all rolled into one.

The rule that seems to operate in most families is that special privilege belongs to the person who makes the (most) money. And one of those privileges is that of determining how the money will be spent.

In my (Dick's) survey of suburban couples, I noted an interesting but not surprising phenomenon. Wives who were employed full-time were most likely to report that they managed the family's finances. Wives who worked part-time were somewhat less frequently in charge of the money. And full-time housewives were least likely of all to be the primary money managers.

Family sociologists Reuben Hill and Robert Becker put the matter bluntly: "Money is a source of power that supports male dominance in the family. . . . Money belongs to him who earns it, not to her who spends it, since he who earns it may withhold it."[3]

This principle was brought home to me when my wife stopped working at our daughter's birth. One of the first questions she asked me was, "Will you put me on an allowance now?" She was used to making her own money and managing ours, so she feared the prospect of being treated like a child with an allowance. Instead, she remained in control of the family finances and never had to worry about an allowance.

Of course, it is well documented that money is a big factor in marital happiness. Much conflict occurs over how money is spent. When wives begin working this conflict might actually decrease.

One reason for this may be obvious: the family now has more money to spend so conflict does not have to arise as often. But there also seems to be a curious correlation between marital adjustment and *who* manages the money. In our study of a hundred married couples, we used a particular professional index (Locke-Wallace) to indicate the level of marital adjustment. Couples had to tell how satisfied they each were with the marriage, the extent of disagreements, the frequency of thoughts of divorce, and the extent of agreements on issues such as child care, sex, and money.

We found that in marriages where the wife managed the

money (families where the wife also tended to work), well over half (57 percent) of the couples had above-average scores in marital adjustment. But only about twenty percent of the couples whose money was managed by the husband enjoyed this degree of happiness.

Why this difference? Our research does not give us grounds for drawing conclusions. But perhaps we can speculate a bit. Harriet and Frank may have some of the answers: "Before Harriet started working at the local supermarket," says Frank, "she would usually check with me before buying something. Now, when she sees a new blouse she'd like to have, chances are she'll buy it and I won't even know it. Do I mind it? Not really. In fact, since Harriet started working, we have less financial pressure. I'm glad she can spend a little more freely. I do, too. And now Harriet manages all our money."

Part of Frank and Harriet's happiness lies in the fact that both now have more money to spend. But just as important is the fact that both now have more independent control over some money. In the past Harriet felt that even decisions on personal items of clothing like a blouse had to be checked with Frank. Now she feels the freedom to decide for herself.

Another possible reason that couples might find more happiness when the wife works and manages the money has to do with decision making. When husbands manage the money, some of them might tend to leave their wives out of the decision-making process. They have been brought up to take control and not to talk extensively about issues. So, some men, especially if they are the sole breadwinner, will give their wives a small allowance and maintain complete control over all the other family money.

When the wife handles the money, on the other hand, she might be more inclined to discuss decisions with her spouse. They end up making major decisions together, and that strengthens the marriage.

When Careers Collide

Ron Gunther is a program director for a local radio station. His wife, Mary, after teaching for two years at their sons' grade school, has just been offered a tenured position at the school. However, Ron has also been offered a new job—in another state. Ron is very interested in this offer; it's a big, new opportunity for him. But Mary now has a stake in her job. What should they do?

When couples develop two careers—when both are intensely invested in their work—conflict can arise when it comes to advancement. In the past, companies seldom worried about families when they wanted to relocate employees. But with more wives working, they have to consider the possibility that the husband won't take the relocation because his wife doesn't want to leave her job. Or maybe it's the wife they're considering relocating! Either way, companies are just beginning to face the issue of how to make relocation attractive to two-career couples.

Married couples need to face the issue of what they will do when such conflicts arise. Some couples simply assume that the husband's job will take precedence. This is especially common if the husband makes substantially more money than the wife. In some cases, however, they might decide the other way around.

One husband we know stayed in a rather stressful job in the plastics industry rather than forcing his wife to leave her job so they could relocate. His reasoning was that, even though his job paid more, hers made a more important contribution to society. She worked for a Christian publishing company and was responsible for developing significant new book topics and authors.

Other couples try to take turns in getting their education and in having satisfying jobs. Typically, the wife will put her husband through school and then he will look for a job near the school she wants to attend. He will put her through school and she will then look for a good job. If he's just spent several years in a very good job, then maybe he will agree to relocate so that she can accept a particularly satisfying opportunity.

All these are solutions that have been tried by various couples. Some even live in two different cities and see each other on weekends (but we don't recommend that). The important thing is that these couples make career decisions together. Once again, communication becomes the key to avoiding major conflict.

Divorce

As soon as we begin talking about the sources of conflict that two-income couples face, the big question that arises is, does a wife's working lead to divorce? In the previous pages we've recognized that a woman's working can put added stress on the marriage. So it is not unreasonable to assume that this added stress can lead to divorce. Is this the case?

Indeed, nationally the divorce rates for employed women are higher than those for full-time housewives.[4] In our interviews of the mostly Christian residents of a Chicago suburb, we found that few women had even considered divorce. But of those that had, a significantly higher number were working wives.

Experts are divided on just what these numbers mean. Some believe that the divorce rates are indeed higher as a direct result of the woman's work. The conflicts are too great for some marriages.

However, others believe that what these statistics show is that working gives a woman an added measure of freedom or security that allows her to get out of an already bad marriage. The conditions for divorce might well exist before the wife begins to work, but once she is gainfully employed the woman feels more capable of surviving on her own without her breadwinner husband. One study seems to bear this out because it showed that significant numbers of women obtain work in order to prepare themselves for divorce.[5]

One thing is clear: working couples face special problems. If the marriage was strong before the wife went to work, then often the marriage will grow even stronger through these new changes and challenges and opportunities. But if the marriage was already in trouble—if communication was minimal, if decisions were not made in partnership, and if traditional roles were an important part of the spouses' identities—then working could well push that marriage closer to the edge.

Jesus warned us to count the cost before we take on a project (Lk 14:28-30). So married couples ought to count the cost when they consider major changes in their lives, such as the wife's going to work or the husband making a major career move. Couples should be prepared to face and resolve the conflicts that will arise. If their marriage is not yet strong enough to handle added stress, then they should not make such major changes.

7

TRUE GUILT AND FALSE

I WAS A GRADE SCHOOL TEACHER AND ENJOYED IT. AFTER my children were born, I stopped working full-time and took substitute teaching instead. However, I really did very little even of that. There were years when I did not work at all. Then when my children were nine and older, I developed an interest in early childhood education and started taking courses to get my certification. I did some part-time teaching at a nursery school at the same time. Finally, last year, I got certified and began working in a nursery school thirty hours per week. I really felt good about myself. I had accomplished something in my midlife and was using it to benefit others. My family enjoyed having the extra income I was bringing in, too."

Life was going very well for Jane, whose husband had a good job and was in favor of her working. But then one of her teenagers, Emily, began having trouble both at school and at home. So Jane and Emily went to see a counselor.

"You should quit all outside activities, including teaching nursery school and Sunday school," said the counselor. "Don't work again until you get your family under control. After all, you don't really need to work."

Women and Guilt

Would the counselor have said that to Jane's husband if he had been the one to bring in a child with a problem? Would he have been asked to quit his job? Would he have had to cut out his other activities, like the Saturday golf games and the monthly fishing trips?

This counselor played on a big part of what it means to be a working mother—feeling guilty. He used that guilt to convince Jane to quit her job. Now that Jane has quit, some things have improved with Emily but more still needs to change. Yet at least Jane doesn't feel guilty that her work is what is causing Emily's problems.

Guilt is a fact of life for most women. They often feel guilty for things that are not wrong. There's a lot of guilt possible in family matters. Whenever something doesn't go just right, Mom can feel guilty. When someone isn't happy, Mom feels responsible. Guilt affects women—working and nonworking—more than men.

Women are brought up to view themselves as nurturers. When they are young, they are taught to take care of others' needs. And when they marry and have children they take on a tremendous sense of responsibility for their family's happiness. When something is amiss, it is almost always the mother who takes action first. Even if the problem is not her fault, she will often feel guilty if she does not do everything in her power to correct it. Research has shown that women tend to feel they are doing something wrong if they are acting to meet their own needs when the needs of others in their family are not completely met. Men do not feel this way.[1]

The working mother feels special guilt. She assumes the role of primary care giver, just like other mothers. But when she begins to work, that role of primary care giver doesn't change. She just adds to it her job responsibilities. Whenever the two sets of demands on her time clash, as they inevitably do, she feels guilty and torn. Our traditional expectations of women (as the primary care givers) have not changed, but the reality of life for most mothers has—most mothers now work.

The double burden of working mothers is almost unavoidable, both because society is not very accommodating of the needs of two-earner families and because the needs for care of the children still fall primarily on the mother.

A woman who is trying to combine work and parenting has to deal with this issue of guilt. She has to learn how to separate true guilt from false guilt. In this chapter we would like to look at forms of guilt to help women decide if their guilt is deserved or not. The first issue to look at is choice. The next is motivation. We'd also like to look at guilt from the standpoint of the Christian community.

Choice and Guilt

On the day after Alice's surgery she was experiencing much pain and nausea. The doctor ordered a pain reliever, but it made Alice very drowsy. She struggled to stay awake when her children, including Grant, her fifteen year old, came to visit.

"I tried very hard not to fall asleep and to be alert so I could visit with them. But it was a losing battle. I feel badly about that, especially for Grant because he tends to get scared and worried. I wanted them all to know that I was fine."

How typical! Alice was feeling guilty for having been too sick to stay awake. She was ignoring her own needs and trying to fulfill the needs of her kids, even from her hospital bed. She had no choice in this matter of staying alert or not, so she was not truly guilty of doing something wrong. Yet she felt bad.

When I kidded Alice about this, she said, "It's part of a mother's instinct, I suppose, to be worried about your children when you should be more concerned about yourself!" It really is not instinct, though (at least not *just* instinct). It is, rather, due more to the fact that women have internalized society's expectations that they will be primarily responsible for their children's total welfare.

Of course, parents *should* be responsible for their children's welfare. But interestingly, it is the parents who take that responsibility most seriously who tend to blame themselves most when circumstances are not perfect.

> Some parents are overbusy because they are too keen on money or fame. . . . Other parents are exhausted trying to make ends meet. A flood of articles addressed to the former asking them whether money and fame are more important than children may never be read by the very parents who should read them. But you can be sure they *will* be read by those in the latter group who are too weary to do more than keep their children fed, clothed and shepherded between school, table, bathroom and bed. Yet the pious articles tell them that if they are too busy to play with their children, then they are too busy. And what shall we say to the widowed, the divorced and the single parents?[2]

If a person is to be held truly guilty for the results of a particular behavior, he or she must have had a choice about the actions. If a mother is too busy out of true necessity, she cannot be held responsible for the consequences—which may not be bad anyway. If a woman is doing her best to meet the needs of her family and things still go wrong, can she be blamed? No.

Instead of guilt the thousands of mothers who work in order to help provide financially for their families ought to feel good about themselves. They ought not feel apologetic for working.

Motivation

But what about the mothers who do not need to work but still choose to do so? Should they feel guilty?

Working for financial reasons, even if just to obtain a certain degree of financial freedom or an extra measure of comfort, is not in itself wrong. The extra income can do much good for the family. And there is nothing necessarily wrong with wanting to lay aside something for the future, either.

However, there is a thin line between wanting a bit more and discontentment. One young couple I know found out how easy it was to slip from working hard for a noble goal to living only for the future. Dan and Debbie married young. They have two children. Although they had waited a couple of years to have children, Dan's income as a salesclerk was not enough to enable them to save towards the down payment for a home. So Debbie went to work as a school-bus driver. And when they changed apartments they left a lot of things in boxes because they were looking forward to the time they would move into a house.

One day, caught between desiring to stay home with her children more and the need to work, Debbie realized that she wasn't even enjoying what time she did have with the children. And the children weren't able to enjoy their home because so many of their things were still packed in boxes. So Debbie finally brought out all the things she had been saving to be used in a new house. And she cut down her hours so she could relax and enjoy her family more. She and Dan are still saving for their own home. But the dream has been put off in favor of having more enjoyment now.

What about women who work because they want the stimulation of adult company? Or those who work to stay in touch with developments in a technical field? Or for a sense of personal satisfaction? Many people feel that a mother who wants more than children and a husband is being selfish. There must be something wrong with her if she cannot be satisfied with her domestic roles. What more could one ask than to have a loving husband who provides well for his family and children who become your pride and joy?

Is it wrong to work for personal satisfaction, mental stimulation and interpersonal contacts? If a woman is bored at home is it selfish for her to go out to work? Must all women try to find fulfillment inside the home? Or is it okay for some women to seek that outside the home if that's where her interests take her?

Women must remember that it is not wrong to try to meet one's own legitimate needs. Satisfaction with life is a legitimate need. And for some women, those whose interests and preferences lie outside the domestic sphere, fulfillment will not be found at home alone. So becoming involved in a job can be a way of meeting a legitimate personal need. While the mother, like the father, should pay attention to how much time and energy her job is taking, there is no moral reason why she should be confined to the home. Unfortunately, however, many Christians try to put such moral responsibility on women.

The Christian Community: Blessing or Curse?

While society is ambivalent at best over working mothers, parts of the Christian community are downright hostile to mothers who work. Even single mothers, who have no choice about working for a living, are not supported and encouraged in some churches as they should be.

Nancy is forty-one years old. She has worked all her adult life, partly because her husband wants her to. She has one child in high school. Her paycheck pays for the family groceries and the child's expenses. Because she had little training, she has been forced to take jobs she did not enjoy just to have the income. But now that her child is in high school, she has enrolled in some college courses to get extra training while still working part-time. She would like to become a counselor for women and troubled youth.

Despite her devotion to her family and to serving others, an elder in her church said to her one day, "Why are you going to school? You should be spending your spare time discipling other women" (referring to the biblical statements in Titus 2:3-5). Because Nancy's activities do not fit the traditional mold, this elder has missed the fact that she has spent her life trying to help provide for her family and that she now hopes to help other women and children in a more professional way. Her life typifies the virtues mentioned in the Scripture to which he alluded, but he cannot see it because Nancy does not fit the image of the ideal Christian homemaker.

Other women, including myself, have faced similar experiences in the church. One year after I left college teaching, I admitted publicly in church to having a sense of deprivation at losing my career. After the service a leading man in the church came up to me and said, "Bee-Lan, it's the devil!" He expressed concern that I was not satisfied in my homemaking role. "Your job is your family," he said. He was afraid I would suddenly pick up and go out to look for another job.

For some members of society and the church women do not have a right to satisfying work. According to these people, women do not share the same rights as men nor the same needs. Fortunately this view is becoming less common. But it still remains, and it makes many women feel uncomfortable with their nondomestic roles. It makes them feel undeservedly guilty.

What's Good for Mom . . .

The truth is, as we've said all along, that what is good for Mom also tends to be good for the family. The happiest families are those where the mothers are happy with their chosen roles, whether staying at home or going out to work. More satisfied women tend to raise better-adjusted children and have healthier marriages.

Women who are active and have many different interests, in particular, tend to be more mentally alert and emotionally stable if they work. Some studies have even shown that they are healthier! Researchers at the University of Michigan examined data from a national health survey and discovered that being employed was positively connected with a woman's physical health.[3]

Peggy Thoits of Princeton University found that improved health often follows adding a new role—for example, working—rather than the other way around.[4] Taking on a new commitment like volunteer work, going back to school or working enhances one's self-esteem and sense of well being. Women with more roles—wife, mother, worker, church volunteer, for example—feel more competent and proud of their achievements. They report feeling more interested and satisfied with their lives than women who have fewer roles.

This does not mean, however, that women who prefer not to work should rush out to find jobs in order to improve their health and self-esteem. The crucial element in a woman's well-being is whether she is doing what she wants to do. Did she have a choice in what she is doing? Professors Ross, Mirowsky and Huber of the University of Illinois studied over 600 women and found that the most depressed group were those who wanted to work outside the home but did not.[5]

In *Mothers Who Work*, the authors report on their survey of working mothers across the nation. An overwhelming majority of the women stated that working had a positive effect on their own emotional well-being, their marriages, and their children. This was especially true of women who worked for personal satisfaction, but also true even among women who worked primarily for economic reasons.[6]

Yet what about all the stress involved in carrying the dual responsibilities of work and parenting? Isn't that bad for a woman and therefore bad for her family? No. Stress is not always bad. In fact, stress is simply a fact of life. Our goal is not to have stress-free lives, but to effectively handle the stress we have—stress that keeps us alert and challenged. If women are doing what they want to do, are busy with things they enjoy, and are being encouraged in their responsibilities, then they will find their lives full of health and vitality. And they will be better parents.

A college classmate of mine once expressed well what it means to carry a lot of responsibilities—have a lot of stress—and to enjoy it. She was manager of the Women's Choral Society at school, captain of the varsity swim team, helped cook for her housemates, and maintained good grades. She said to me one day, "It is a good feeling to go to bed tired after a hard day."

If a mother can have a satisfying job—if that's what she

chooses—and also know that her children are well cared for, she could well be a better mother and wife. On the other hand, if she does not see to it that her own needs are met, she may discover that she is harboring resentful feelings towards her family. Therefore, one need not feel guilty about having a fulfilling life-style, because it ends up being good for the family too.

In the next section we will offer advice on how a woman who chooses to work outside the home can best juggle all her responsibilities and remain a happy, healthy, effective mom.

PART III

HELP FOR MOMS WHO CHOOSE TO WORK

8

FINDING SUBSTITUTE CHILD CARE

MY TWO OLDER CHILDREN SAY THAT THEY HAVE THREE grandmothers—my mother, my mother-in-law, and the older lady who used to care for them when I worked outside the home. They called her "Grams," and they still remember her well.

I was very lucky to find someone special to come to my home to care for my children. Each week Grams and I would discuss plans for the week to come. On days when I did not get home at the expected time, she would wait patiently for me to come. She always respected my wishes for the children, even though some of them may not have made sense to her (and she was much more experienced in child rearing than I).

She gave our kids undivided attention. Even if I had not worked, I don't think I would've spent hours in the rocking chair by the window with the baby, reading aloud to him when he was just a few months old. I attribute his early reading ability to Grams's attentiveness!

The Alternatives

Finding substitute care for your children is probably the most difficult decision a working parent faces. Many mothers fret about it at length and then end up taking the first possibility they find just because they're afraid they won't find anything else.

Other couples try various methods to avoid using substitute

care at all. One alternative is to work staggered schedules. Perhaps Dad works the night shift at the factory while Mom works the day shift at the supermarket. Or maybe Mom works part-time while the kids are in school. Perhaps the parents have employers that allow flexible schedules and they can work things out—especially if one of them is part-time—to avoid hired child care. That is quite possible in highly independent work such as that of college professors or some ministers. And, of course, people who are in business for themselves often have this luxury of flexible schedules.

Many mothers choose to work part-time or seek employers that allow flex-time in order to minimize the need for substitute child care. But such arrangements, especially flex-time, are still rare. Most employers want their workers to report in at certain hours and to be available during a standard work day or shift.

Couples who deliberately work different shifts in order to be home with their children seem to have something of an ideal situation. This might be true if one person works part-time and thus is only away a couple of days or nights per week. But if both parents work full-time on different shifts, they may see their kids a lot, but they seldom see each other. When one spouse is at home with the children the other is either at work or sleeping. This makes it exceedingly difficult to maintain good communication and a sense of togetherness.

Other mothers try to do two things at once. They stay home with their children and work at the same time. Often these women are self-employed or work in cottage industries. Computer technology has made this more possible these days because women can now be linked to an office through a home computer and a phone.

But women who both work and take care of their children are either themselves exceptional or have exceptional children. It is a rare preschooler who will entertain herself or himself for an hour or more at a time. Some mothers use the television set to entertain the kids, yet that is anything but ideal. At best, a work-at-home mother faces constant interruptions. If her work requires strong concentration (such as computer work as opposed to more routine tasks like stuffing envelopes), it will be hard for her to handle these intrusions.

If a mother has to talk on the phone, working with a child at home is probably nearly impossible. Many children have a habit of demanding attention as soon as Mom picks up the receiver. Of course, they can be trained not to interrupt as they grow older. But how many mothers would want to try to carry on business—talk to a customer, for instance—with a screaming baby in the background? And how many mothers have left their home offices for a minute to check on something only to return to a disaster zone that's just been invaded by a toddler?

At least one survey of mothers of preschool children who worked at home found that half of these mothers had to find substitute child care for their children to make working feasible.[1]

A Baby-Sitter at Your Home

If you find that your working requires substitute care, what are your choices? Essentially they are three: a baby-sitter who comes to your home, a sitter who takes children into her home, or a day-care center.

Grams was our in-home baby-sitter. She came to my house each day that I worked and cared for our boys. She fed them, played with them, and cleaned up after them.

The advantages of this kind of care are obvious. When a sitter comes to your house, you don't have to get the children dressed and fed and packed into the car before you can leave for work. You can simply walk out the door and leave everything—including sleeping children—to the sitter. And you are guaranteed, if your sitter is competent, that your kids will receive adequate attention. There are no other children to distract her.

But there are disadvantages to this type of care. The most

obvious is the expense. Not only do you have to pay an in-home sitter substantially more than a center, but you are also responsible for paying social security and unemployment taxes for that person (and going to the bother of filing periodic tax reports). The minimum expense would be minimum wage, but most sitters get more than that, especially if they also do some light housework. While the taxes and a portion of the pay can be used (at present) to reduce your income taxes, the cost is still much higher than other forms of care. Because of that, most parents don't even consider this type of care until they have more than one child needing it. Such sitters are also difficult to find.

Some two-career couples actually hire a live-in nanny rather than just a sitter. This person, of course, is even more expensive since you provide room and board along with a substantial salary. But some professional couples are able to afford this. Anita and Rick both taught college and so had a fairly high income. When Anita's friend, Mary, was divorced, Anita asked her to move in and act as a nanny for the children. Whenever the parents weren't home Mary would take control of the household and the kids.

Other moms and dads are lucky enough to have a relative to care for their children. Grandma or Aunt Susan might make an excellent sitter and give your kids the opportunity of being especially close to their extended family. But you must be careful not to abuse your privilege as a family member. You should not neglect to spell out your expectations for your child's care. You should also treat relatives with the same courtesy that you would give to anyone else. You should inform them of schedule changes in advance and not expect them to show up on a moment's notice. And you should also pay them, or at least offer to do so.

What kinds of traits is it important for a baby-sitter to have? The answer to this question was brought home to me when I met the two sitters a friend used.

Fran is a businesswoman who has separated from her husband. Her three preschool children are usually cared for by Tammy, a mother who brings her own four year old with her to Fran's house.

I once had occasion to leave my four year old with Tammy and the kids during the day. When I returned my boy was having such a good time he didn't want to leave. The older kids were all gathered around the kitchen table coloring with paint and markers while the baby looked on.

But when Tammy wasn't available, Fran used another sitter, an eighteen year old named Barbara. Fran's five year old once said, "I don't like it when Barbara baby-sits us. She doesn't let us play. She yells and screams at us if we play with each other, and she tells us to go and watch TV. She wants us to watch television all the time!"

I realized that, perhaps because Barbara is not a parent herself, she just didn't seem to know how to handle three active boys. To her, loud and rambunctious play seemed like misbehaving. She found that the only time the boys were quiet and manageable was when they were watching TV.

So when looking for a sitter, you should look for someone who is reliable and experienced. And you've got to find someone who loves children, or else that person is going to make maintaining order the highest priority at the expense of freedom and playfulness. At the end of this chapter we've offfered some general guidelines for finding good substitute care.

Family Day Care

That same principle applies when you are looking for someone to take your child into her home. Family day care, as this is usually called, is the most common type of substitute care. Across the country there are thousands of women who care for several children (usually along with their own kids) in their homes.

One of the advantages of this type of care is that it provides a warm, homey setting for your kids while being quite a bit less expensive than hiring someone to come to your house. You don't have to pay social security or unemployment taxes for such a sitter, as she is considered self-employed.

Since infants need a lot of special attention and care, most parents who can't afford to have a sitter come to them choose care in someone else's home. It seems more personal than an institutional setting, and that's especially important for babies. Some parents find sitters who will take in only one or two other children, thus giving the kids plenty of attention.

Another advantage of family day care is that it gives your child playmates other than siblings. After age one, playing with other children becomes an important learning experience. Toddlers interact with one another and learn how other children respond to them. Pediatrician Berry Brazelton writes: "A toddler at home can be pretty lonely without siblings or peers. I used to keep a list of toddlers in my office so isolated mothers . . . could . . . get their children together and relieve the boredom for both parent and child."[2]

However, while some home day-care situations can be ideal, others are less so. Some day-care homes (usually those caring for more than two or three children) are licensed by the state. These licensing procedures usually guarantee minimum standards of safety and quality but little beyond that. And often it is the licensed homes which have the highest number of children being cared for by just one adult.

Dr. Brazelton recommends that there be no more than three infants, four toddlers or five older preschoolers to one adult. But some day-care homes are host to five, eight, even ten children at a time of varying ages. This might be okay for school-age children or older preschoolers, but infants and toddlers need more attention than a woman can give who has seven others to care for.

Thus, when you check out a possible day-care home, you need to look for a situation where your child will be treated like an individual and given individual attention, rather than simply given "maintenance" care—feeding, changing, dressing, etc. You want a sitter who will play with your kids and provide interesting things for them to do.

You should check the safety precautions in a day-care home. Look for covered electrical outlets, gates guarding stairways, electrical cords kept out of the way, and so on. Also, check out how clean the house is, what kinds of play equipment are available, and the provisions for outdoor play. Ask about the sitter's policies on medical checkups, sick children and vacations, how she handles emergencies, and what a typical day at her home is like. (For more suggestions on how to interview baby-sitters, you might want to get a book from the library. Several recent publications include lots of practical advice for working parents. One such volume is *The Working Parents Survival Guide* by Sally Wendkos Olds New York: Bantam Books, 1983.)

Day-Care Centers

A third common form of day care is the institutional type, a day-care center. These come in all different forms. Some only take children who are potty trained while others take infants from birth up. Some provide a teaching environment for children, including trying to teach preschoolers to read, while others are more oriented toward just allowing children to play together. Some centers have received very bad publicity because of child abuse, but most are run by underpaid but well-meaning people.

Like the other forms of day care, centers have both advantages and disadvantages. As you might guess, one advantage is cost. These tend to be the least expensive form of day care, although prices vary a great deal from center to center and from state to state.

Like the family day-care home, a center also provides your child with an opportunity to play with peers. And the best-run centers (including most of the large chains of centers) will provide structured activities to teach age-appropriate lessons. Through play children can learn basic lessons about the world, language, numbers, themselves and others. Most centers do more structured learning activities and more craft or art projects than a sitter would do with your kids. And most require that staff have some formal training in early childhood education.

Some places, called early learning centers, try to accelerate learning by teaching preschoolers to read and manipulate numbers. But these are somewhat controversial because children can get burned out on learning when they have been started on advanced material at an early age.

Another advantage is that the center can be more reliable than a single individual. The center is always open on workdays, even when one or more staff are off sick. You won't get a call at 7 a.m. telling you that you have to keep your child home that day because the sitter is sick. Likewise, day-care centers don't take vacations or develop personal problems that affect their work.

The major disadvantage of a day-care center is the number of staff. The staff to child ratio should be quite low for infants and young children (as noted in the previous section), but most centers can't afford to hire that many staff and still charge a reasonable, competitive rate. The worst centers are understaffed by people who have little training or love for children. In such a setting infants, in particular, are vulnerable. Infants fail to thrive when they are not adequately stimulated by someone's cuddling, talking and playing with them. Simply changing diapers and feeding the infants in assembly line fashion can be very detrimental.

Because of this danger, many parents try to avoid taking small infants to day-care centers, preferring family homes or in-home help instead. However, there are some centers that manage to provide adequate care for even the littlest charges.

Another disadvantage can be the staff turnover. The Labor Department has found that the day-care industry has one of the highest employee turnover rates of all, about forty percent annually. This is due largely to difficult working conditions, low pay and minimal benefits. Although the worst situation for a child is to be moved from one new day-care situation to another (for example, from a home to a center and then back to a different home again), attending a center with constant staff changes is not good either.

Studies of children from eighteen months to three years of age indicate that those whose day-care providers have changed several times show less self-control and less confidence than peers in more stable environments.[3] So parents should aim for finding the most stable environment possible and sticking with it. Day-care centers with extremely high turnover rates (which can be discovered by asking several staff members how long they have worked there) should be avoided because of this instability and the possibility that staff are unhappy. Disgruntled staff will not provide the best care.

If you are considering using a day-care center, check it out well. Do they encourage unannounced parental visits? Do they welcome volunteer help from parents? What kinds of activities are planned for each day? Is there adequate time for meals, rest and quiet activities such as story time? What qualifications do staff have? Are staff mature and experienced or are they inexperienced teens? Again, the books on the market for working parents provide a wealth of information on how to find the highest quality care. It's up to you to take the time to do so.

Investigating Substitute Care

No matter what type of care you choose for your child, you need to carefully check out several possible situations before you choose one. A key part of that process is the interview with the prospective sitter or center director and staff.

Jean began interviewing Betty, a family day-care provider, asking questions about the types of things the children did during the day. Suddenly Betty stopped the interview and refused to continue.

"No one else has ever asked me all these questions. You

must not have to work. The people who bring their kids here don't have any choice." Betty was intimidated by the interview questions (standard ones derived from *The Working Parents Survival Guide*). None of the other parents had ever taken the care to ask such things.

That episode was a sad commentary on the methods parents use to find child care. After fretting about the decision for weeks, many parents do not allow themselves enough time to make the best decision. Jean stopped interviewing Betty and went on to interview three more possible workers during her three-week search for child care. The situation she eventually decided on was excellent. Here are some general principles to follow in such a search.

1. Give yourself time. You don't have to take the first sitter you find, unless you have not allowed yourself enough time to look around. In most areas, there are still plenty of choices about day care as long as you allow yourself a few weeks to research the possibilities.

2. Investigate the prospects. Word of mouth is still probably the best way to find good care. Through friends, acquaintances, relatives, and co-workers you may hear of an excellent situation that comes highly recommended. For example, many of the most stable environments are the homes of middle-aged women who take in just a couple of children and do not carry state licenses. They do it because they love kids, but they don't advertise. Yet many of them are gems.

Also ask what the going rates are for the various types of care. Higher cost may sometimes mean better care, but not necessarily.

3. Check references. In addition to interviewing several possible sitters or center staff members, also get a list of references. Try to talk to the parents of children currently under that person's care. Find out how they like the care their kids receive. If you know of someone who has removed their child from that day-care situation, find out why.

4. Let her interact with your child. Visit the family day-

care home with your child or have the sitter visit you when your child is present. How do they respond to each other? Does the woman naturally seem to gravitate toward kids, or does she ignore your child while you are together?

5. Clarify hours and duties as well as pay. Make your expectations clear and find out hers. What happens when she goes on vacation or is sick? What if you are late picking up your child? Will your in-home sitter also do housework?

6. Ease into the new setting. If you possibly can, try out a new situation for a few days, at first leaving your child for just a short time.

7. Maintain open communication. Be honest if some aspect of your child's care doesn't suit you, and invite honesty in return. If you're a young mother dealing with an experienced mom, don't be afraid to ask for advice.

8. Avoid making a big issue out of insignificant differences in care. There are bound to be things that you would like done differently with your child. And you might even face some feelings of jealousy toward the person who cares for your infant. Try not to let those feelings govern your behavior. Decide what is most important to you—attentiveness, warmth, cleanliness, safety, for example—and then make up your mind to grin and bear the little things that might get under your skin—maybe the fact that she folds the diapers in a triangle rather than a square, gives your child Spaghetti O's or alfalfa sprouts for lunch three days a week, or lets her dog lick your baby's face. If it's not a crucial issue, it's probably not worth getting upset about if the general care your child gets is competent and loving. Choose your battles!

9. Stay in touch. Once you've chosen a sitter or center, be alert for how your child is responding. Talk to the sitter about what your child's days are like. Drop in unexpectedly to see what goes on in your absence. And take seriously any indications that your child is consistently unhappy.

Finding good day care is an extremely difficult task. But if you put time and energy into it you will probably be rewarded with someone who can complement your own skills and values. Although children do indeed prefer their mothers most of the time, alternative care can stimulate and enrich your child if that care is good. It's worth looking for the best!

Care for Older Children

School-age children whose parents work daytime hours need to be watched by someone else after school ends. While some public school districts and private schools have begun instituting extended days—substitute care after the regular school day ends—this is still the exception. Further, these school districts still provide nothing during the summertime when children need supervision all day long.

Most working parents try to line up a neighbor or friend to watch their children after school. Many children walk or ride to school with friends who live nearby. Perhaps the ideal is for the children to be able to go to a friend's house and to be supervised by that friend's mother who is paid for her services a couple of hours each day.

But what seems ideal can be difficult to work out in practice. Kids sometimes change friends as often as they change clothes. What do you do about after-school care when Kathy suddenly decides that she despises her former friend, Mary? And how many neighbors and friends will agree to watch your kids all day long during the summer? Not many. Often that means that in the summertime working parents resort to using high school and college students to provide day care at home. Yet most such kids want jobs that pay more than baby-sitting, and many students are not mature enough to do a good job caring for youngsters all day.

Many women who take in young children for day care also will watch older children after school. Then the trick is finding a good sitter located within walking distance of your child's school or along your child's bus route. If you find such a person, then you also need to see if she will watch your children all day during the summer months.

Day-care centers can be a help both after school and during summers. Many of them have van services which drop children off at local schools in the morning (for parents who begin their workdays early) and pick them up again in the afternoon. Some of the best centers also have special all-day programs for older children during the summer. These are often run like day camps, with lots of field trips, outdoor activities and crafts. Such programs can be rather expensive, however.

But the most difficult decisions arise when your children get older. Some ten and twelve year olds, and most teens, want nothing to do with day-care centers and neighborhood sitters. Yet, especially in the summertime when their days are free, they can easily fill in boring time with dangerous activities or sibling fights.

"Latchkey kids," as such children are called, have become a major national concern. It is estimated that from 2 to 7 million children (about one-fourth of all school-age kids) come home to empty houses after school. When these children become victims of crime or neglect—or begin to commit crimes themselves—then national attention is again focused on the problem.

Generally speaking, it is not good to put a child in a situation where he or she might be unsafe, feel insecure or helpless, or be lonely. But saying this does not mean that any parent who leaves a child alone before or after school is negligent. We should not be automatically prejudiced against all parents of "latchkey kids."

Laura and Adam leave their children alone for a short time before school some days. Adam is a computer programmer who lives 45 minutes away from his work in Boston. Laura is a nurse working three nights per week. They have a boy and girl, ages nine and eight.

Adam leaves for work at 7:45 each morning. The kids leave for school at 8:15, and when Laura works she doesn't get home until 8:30. What happens in those 30 minutes the kids spend alone?

Adam and Laura have provided well for their kids, so chaos doesn't break out when they're unsupervised. Visiting them, I was impressed by how smoothly things ran. Laura packs lunches the night before and Adam makes sure that the lunches and schoolbooks are stacked by the door in the morning. Their aunt stops by and picks up the children for school when she is taking her own there. The two kids seem well-adjusted and happy, not threatened by the responsibility of getting themselves out the door on some school mornings.

Organization and maturity are perhaps two key factors in whether children can successfully be left to care for themselves. In most cases, it's the parents who have to be organized. Even if the children are fully responsible to take care of themselves—and perhaps even make meals—the parents still have to have things somewhat prepared so this can happen.

Your child's maturity, along with the kind of neighborhood you live in and how long the kids are unsupervised, is the most important issue for you to consider. Some children will be intimidated by responsibility. They will be frightened by being alone and unsure of how to behave. Other children rise to the occasion, developing self-assurance and confidence as a result of having extra responsibility. One thirteen year old said to researchers, "I really feel good that my parents trust me enough to take care of myself after school. I know it is a big responsibility but I think I'm old enough."[4] Some even older children, however, may lack the maturity this girl shows and should not be left alone.

Only you can decide whether your child is ready for such independence. But be sure to talk it over with him, too. Ask him what he thinks of it, how he would feel, and what possible problems he can foresee. If you all feel ready, then give it a try with the understanding that you may have to change the decision if it doesn't work out.

Teenagers who do not need sitters still need to know that someone is available to them. You might find that if a neighbor is willing to be available to your teen after school, that neighbor might develop a special relationship with your child just when your child needs adult confidants. The child who has an adult to whom he can talk openly and honestly is indeed fortunate. And so are the parents. When parental relations become strained, as is at times inevitable during the teen years, your child will still have a mature person to talk to about important matters.

Also, prepare your child well for the experience. Does she know what to do in an emergency? What neighbor can she call for help if she needs it? What would she do if a stranger came to the door? Have you set up specific guidelines for having friends over or playing outside? Are there chores you want the kids to do before playtime? *The Working Parent Dilemma* by Earl Grollman and Gerri Sweder has detailed suggestions for children and parents. Your local library will also have a supply of books for kids and parents dealing with all sorts of practical matters related to staying home alone.

Parents should always call their children when they are home alone. Many mothers have regular "check-in" times when they call their kids or their kids call them, such as first thing when the child arrives home from school. The phone call is not only to be sure your child is safe. It is another expression of caring and another opportunity to talk, even though brief.

One thing working parents should try to avoid is giving too much responsibility to older children for baby-sitting younger ones. A friend of mine told of how she used to tyrannize her younger sister when she had to watch her. "I didn't know any other way to make her mind me," Stephanie said. Sibling rivalries can become especially intense when one has authority over the others. Research has even made note of something called the "little mother" syndrome. Some women do not want to become mothers because they carried too much responsibility as a child for younger brothers and sisters.

Clearly, child care for older kids presents some special

problems. But creative parents can usually come up with special solutions that fit their child's needs, desires, and level of maturity.

9

SHARED PARENTING

THIS BOOK HAS BEEN PRIMARILY WRITTEN WITH MOTHERS in mind. They are the ones most likely to read this, though I wish it were otherwise.

That very fact points up a significant problem: fathers are not active enough in the rearing of their children. While most fathers are involved in the decision of whether their wives should work, few of them are active after the fact in trying to solve the problems that Mom's working (or staying at home) creates. What happens in the family should be *everyone's* business, not just Mom's.

Research shows that many children are starved for their fathers' attention.[1] Many of the problems that these children—especially adolescents—have stem not so much from their mothers' work as from their fathers noninvolvement in their lives.

"Children of both sexes and all ages clearly feel that their mothers consistently demonstrate a greater amount of love and affection than do their fathers."[2] This conclusion comes from a careful nationwide study of over one thousand children living with their working parents (published in *The Working Parent Dilemma*). The study quotes one fifteen-year-old girl as saying, "Mothers seem to know that kids need lots of loving: fathers still have to learn that."

We all know that the assurance of having our parents' unconditional love is the foundation for building our self-esteem. What is interesting, however, is that this study found that the degree of contact a child has with his or her father seems to have more impact on self-esteem than contact with mother. Why?

These results do not indicate that children don't need moms. Rather, they point out that there may be less variation in the love and attention that children receive from their mothers. Fathers, on the other hand, vary widely in the amount of care they give their kids. Some dads are great at playing with their children and showing them affection. Others remain extremely distant and cold. Thus, the differences in self-esteem tend to show up in paternal relationships. We should modify the old saying, "Every child needs his mother" to "Every child needs *both* his parents."

When fathers provide for their children by bringing home a paycheck, that's great. But they also need to provide their children with love and discipline. If a mother works, some of her attention may be removed from her kids. But that may be a positive thing if it means that Dad will get more involved in family affairs. Perhaps the wife's working will free Dad up (for example, because he won't need a second job to make ends meet) to spend more time and emotional energy with his children. The problem, however, is that this often is not the case.

Love, Self-Esteem, and Discipline

Self-esteem is basic to the healthy development of persons from childhood to adulthood. Having high self-esteem means that one has a strong sense that one is inherently worthy, loved, and competent. This is not to say that the person with high self-esteem feels perfect or sinless. On the contrary, that person knows that he is loved *in spite of* his shortcomings.

The person with adequate self-esteem is more capable of being a loving person. The sense of being accepted and loved as he is makes him more likely to accept and love others as they are—human and fallible. Good self-esteem also provides one with a sense of confidence and ability to cope with the world. A child with high self-esteem, therefore, will more easily develop independence and a strong sense of responsibility. And these will further build self-esteem.

We often think of discipline as punishment for wrongdoing, but it is much more than that. Discipline should be aimed towards the positive goal of developing a child into a mature and God-pleasing individual. But before any discipline can be effective in meeting this positive goal, it must be grounded in the child's sense of being loved and accepted by her parents. She must understand why she is being disciplined—for her own good and out of the love her parents hold for her.

As Christian parents our discipline ought to be modeled after the discpline of God. The writer of Hebrews described God's discipline this way:

> "My son, do not make light of the Lord's discipline, and do not lose heart when he rebukes you, because the Lord disciplines those he loves, and he punishes everyone he accepts as a son." Endure hardship as discipline; God is treating you as sons. For what son is not discplined by his father? God disciplines us for our good, that we may share in his holiness. (12:5-7, 10)

What should these words tell us about our discipline as human parents? First, that our children must know that they are loved. They need reminders of that love often enough so that they will not forget it when they are being disciplined.

Second, they should know that we discipline them *because* we love them. If we did not care about them then we would not care how they behaved or what happened to them. Likewise, we must look to ourselves to make sure that our discipline is indeed aimed at our child's good. We should avoid using discipline simply to vent our anger or to enforce demands which have more to do with family power politics than love.

Third, discipline includes both punishment and hardship.

God allows us to experience hardship in order to learn lessons. Deuteronomy 32:11 compares God's care to that of a mother eagle. She stirs up the nest and causes the baby eagles to fall out. But she catches them before they are hurt. That is the way they learn to fly.

Likewise, as parents we have to let our children learn from the "school of hard knocks" at times. By facing the consequences of their actions, our children learn what is good to do and what is not. If, after repeated warnings, a child still leaves his bike on the sidewalk and it is stolen, then the lesson that his belongings must be put away becomes one he will never forget. If we protect him, by putting the bike away for him or by replacing the stolen one, we do him no favors. We must in love let him face the consequences.

Communicating both love and limits to our children may take some special efforts from working parents, especially fathers. It may seem obvious, but if you want your children to feel loved *you have to tell them you love them.* Many men, especially those who had silent or distant fathers, find this hard to do. You may have to force yourself sometimes, but you should tell all your children, even older ones, regularly that you love them. You can tell them when you put them to bed, or leave a note for them when you go to work. Or communicate nonverbally (but don't limit yourself to nonverbal communication) by hugging, kissing, or patting your child on the back. Don't get so hurried by your busy life that you neglect this crucial part of parenting.

Second, you should *take time to discipline* your kids. Working parents sometimes find it easier to overlook wrongdoing than to deal with it because it takes effort and time. Further, some mothers feel guilty because they work, and they compensate for that by going easy on their children. But they're not doing them any favors. They're really neglecting their duties, not being extra nice, when they fail to handle bad behavior.

Third, you should *encourage your child's independence.* Don't do things for your youngster just because you're in a hurry and you can do it faster. Your boy or girl needs to learn to do things alone. And your child also needs to contribute to the household by taking responsibility for chores. Working parents can err in either direction when it comes to chores. Either the overworked mother loads too much on her children, or she feels guilty and lets them get away without helping at all. You need to avoid both extremes and give your child age-appropriate tasks to perform, rotating duties that everyone especially dislikes.

Combining Working and Parenting

Time becomes a crucial issue for the working parent. There's no doubt that letting a child know he is loved takes time. And that's at a premium when you work. An important thing you need to get across to your child is that he is more important than your work. But how can you do that consistently? It's going to be difficult.

Working parents need to pay close attention to how they treat those times in their lives when work and kids come into conflict; for example, when a child is sick or when there is a special event taking place during normal work time or in the evening when you're tired.

A parent who is consistently unavailable at crucial times in a child's life will be showing that child that work is the most important thing in Mom's life or Dad's. Do you take time to listen to your daughter's description of the new boy in class? Does your son get your attention when he's unhappy because he did poorly on a test? Does your older child get left home alone when she is sick, even when she is feeling especially ill?

How about those ball games and music recitals? Or teachers' conferences and school open houses? Do you take the time from your busy schedule to make such events a priority? If not, why not? And what does that say to your child?

Your kids can understand if you have occasional busy periods at work that demand your special attention. My boys have had to put up with my working exceptionally hard on this book for several weeks, but they and I know that this is a temporary situation. If, however, you find yourself making excuses on a *regular* basis because you must miss Sharon's swim meet again or Billy's spelling contest, then something is wrong. You need to reexamine your priorities.

Working parents must protect their family lives from being invaded by their work lives. They must keep the two areas separate. Yet, on the other hand, they should try to involve their families in their work. How can you do both?

The Juggling Act

Your children need to know what you do when you work. They need to be able to picture Mom and Dad at their jobs, to know what they do and why, and to be able to feel some pride in their parents. Just as your kids want you to be a part of their lives, so they want to be part of yours. My son, Jason, loves to come into my home office while I'm writing on the computer and stand beside my chair watching. At school he has been learning about how to write and rewrite essays, so he enjoys seeing me do the same. When I print out a chapter I let him tear apart the fan-folded pages. The oldest boy, Stephen, learned more about my kind of work by taking a summer class in journalism in which he visited radio stations and newspaper offices.

Younger children love to talk about what their parents do and teach their friends about it. Many teachers will invite parents to come in and share with the children something about their work. One publishing company was regularly visited by elementary classes that wanted to see what the book business was all about. Some of the children who came to visit had parents working for that company. They were so proud to be able to point out what Mommy or Daddy was doing!

Even if you don't invite your son's entire fourth-grade class along, you still should bring your son to visit your company to show him what you do. Take him to where you work and demonstrate the tasks you perform all day. Or, take your teenaged daughter out to lunch on a day she has off, letting her pick you up at your office or factory.

If your children know something about your work, then they may be able to understand better when you have a bad day and need extra patience from them at home. But, in general, you should try not to bring home from work the negative feelings that may have built up during the day. Try to keep your work and family lives separate enough so that they don't adversely affect each other.

Some parents bring actual work home with them. Dad may fill a briefcase with files and retire to the bedroom after dinner to finish things that he didn't get done in the office. If he—or Mom—has to do that, he should avoid getting the work out before the kids go to bed. Evenings should be family time, not overtime.

Evenings should also be relatively peaceful. If you've had a rotten day on the assembly line, try to vent your feelings before you get home. One child reports, "When my dad has had a hard day at work, he takes his anger out on the rest of us. . . . He'll yell at us for the littlest thing, like talking too loud on the phone. We try staying out of my dad's way as much as possible until he cools down."[3]

Occasional bad days are to be expected, and children must learn the fact of life that parents are people, too and have needs. But if you are regularly losing your cool because of something that happened at work, you need to change jobs or find some way to better cope with your feelings. At the very least, you need to honestly admit your feelings.

Your kids will probably surprise you with how well they can understand a statement like, "Boy, did I have an awful day today. My boss was on my case every minute." After all, your children have days like that, too. But saying that is a far cry from keeping your true feelings inside and saying instead, "How could you be such an idiot as to let the dog chew on the sofa cushion?!"

One study found that 37 percent of children said their working parents were grumpy at the end of the day. This grumpiness comes out when "normal child behavior unexpectedly becomes unacceptable, and parents lash out verbally or mete out swift punishments. Suddenly, the stereo is too loud, a child is too boisterous, or spilling a glass of milk is reckless."[4]

There are as many ways of keeping family and work separate as there are families. Some commuters find their time on the way home helpful for thinking over the day's events and handling the tensions. If your commute is a particularly difficult one, however, the rush-hour traffic will probably not help your peace of mind. But those who are lucky enough to be able to take public transportation may find the commute refreshing. Anita uses her time on the train to catch a short catnap. She gets rid of her tiredness and simultaneously gets geared up to listen to her children. Other parents take a short nap just after returning home.

If dinnertime is a hassle because everyone arrives home at the same time hungry, then you might consider serving snacks or eating dinner in three courses. Try offering hungry family members fruit, a salad, or crackers and cheese to tide them over until the meal is ready. That way, whoever prepares the meal can do so in a leisurely fashion and no one becomes grumpy due to hunger.

Quality Time

Whenever the issue of working parents arises, someone mentions the idea of "quality time." Quality time refers to time that is spent giving relaxed but focused attention to your children. It can include reading stories, playing together or just talking. The point that many working parents make is that while many nonworking mothers spend lots of hours in the same house with their children, they do not necessarily spend much quality time with them.

While no one can say exactly how much quality time a child needs, studies have been done to determine how much time parents spend focusing on their kids. Researchers at the University of Michigan surveyed 1,500 households in 1975 and 922 of the same households in 1981, using detailed diaries to determine how much time working and nonworking mothers spent attending to their kids. [5]

They found that at-home mothers spend about 30 minutes each weekday and 36 minutes each weekend day in quality-time activities with their children. Working mothers clocked some 11 minutes each weekday and 30 minutes on weekend days doing the same. However, in general, the at-home mothers in this study had younger children than the working mothers, so some of the difference in times may be due to that. And, while the at-home mothers may spend more quality time, the times were surprisingly small for both sets of moms. Other studies indicate that the differences in time use between at-home and working moms is not significant at all.[6]

Fathers came out even worse in these studies. In the Michigan study, dads gave 8 minutes per day to their children on weekdays and 14 on weekend days. This was the same for fathers with at-home wives and those whose wives worked. Thus, fathers are not picking up the slack for working wives, which is what one would hope would happen. Instead, "working mothers try to compensate by cutting back on things like sleep and leisure activities," the report says.

The most effective working parents seem to be those who, in a highly organized fashion, regularly schedule time alone with each child every night (just after work or before bed, for example) or each week (special activities together like dinner or backyard games).

One problem, however, is that quality time often can't be planned; it just happens. No one can really predict when those special moments together will occur—the moments that you and the children will remember for a long time. You might have to spend hours and hours together before that one set of events occurs that you will all recall with affection.

That happened to us on a family vacation. We scheduled into our time lots of sightseeing and fun activities. But the most memorable day of the whole week turned out to be the last day, when we all just gave up trying to do things and relaxed instead. We were touring the Grand Tetons in a borrowed camper. That day we had planned on taking an aerial tram ride up a mountain. But after lunch Tim decided to set up a special little tent we had brought along just for the boys. Once this was up, the boys started playing games inside because the tent was a novelty. Since they were occupied, I sat down to read a book.

Later Stephen came looking for me. It turned out that Dad had fallen asleep in the tent and the other two boys were starting to drift off. Only Stephen wasn't tired enough for a nap. He and I instead took the dirty clothes to the washroom, and I gave him his first lesson in the ways of a Chinese hand laundry. We never went to the aerial tram, but we all got some much-needed rest and relaxation. When we returned home, we looked back on that day as one of the highlights of the trip. But who could have predicted it?

Quality time, it seems, can't always be planned. But time with our kids can be planned. And one way to ensure that we're giving them enough of our time is to turn off the TV when we are together. In *The Berenstain Bears and Too Much TV*, Jan and Stan Berenstain tell a story for children that has helpful lessons for adults. When the bear family gets into the habit of watching TV together instead of talking, Mama Bear takes matters into her own hands and puts a moratorium on TV watching for a week. At first the family members don't know what to do with the silence and spare time. But they soon learn to fill it with family conversation and activities. When the moratorium is over, TV no longer holds as much attraction for the Bear family. They have learned to enjoy other things.

The University of Michigan study found that at-home

mothers spend about 8 hours per week watching television *with their children.* Working moms spend about 6 1/2 hours. Is that quality time? Not according to the study. Although watching a program and discussing it can be quality time, just sitting together on the same couch watching the same TV set is not. If working parents are to carve out enough time to focus on their children, they are going to have to cut down on relaxing but ineffective activities like TV watching.

We all have to become better at finding relaxation in doing things that are fun together. Taking walks around the block, making popcorn or other goodies, playing table games, even just roughhousing can all be good quality-time activities. They can be relaxing for a harried mom and dad while still being fun for the kids. As a working parent you will have to work hard at spending precious time with your youngsters. But it will be worth it.

NURTURING THE WORKING MARRIAGE

Author John White has said, "Marriage has something in common with a trapeze act. There is grave risk in both, and neither seems inherently secure. Yet as each partner concentrates on performing his or her movements in the best way possible, a stunning, well-coordinated performance takes place."[1]

In chapter six we looked at just how much of a trapeze act the marriage of two working people can become. As demands on the couple's time and energy increase, coordination becomes so critical that it might seem as though Murphy's Law—if something can go wrong it will—threatens to take over. Sometimes the balance is upset in an instant, as when Mom comes down with flu just two days before Christmas. Other times that balance decays slowly until one day we wake up and realize we're actually teetering on the brink of disaster.

Chapter six discussed some problems that are unique to working couples. In this chapter we would like to look at some ways to prevent having those problems become the foundation of a bad marriage. We examined issues such as housework, money, common values and career coordination. It became clear that underlying these potential hot spots are some basic ways of relating to each other. For example, what tends to determine whether a couple will have conflict over money is not so much who makes the money as who has input into how the money is handled. That involves good communication and open decision making.

We would like to look at identity building, communication and decision making to see how these areas can become critical ones for working spouses.

Building a New Identity

When a wife goes to work the roles in the family no longer strictly fit the stereotype of a breadwinner husband and a homemaker wife. If the husband tries to help out around the house, and if the wife makes a career of her job and brings in a substantial paycheck, then the roles are at times reversed. Dad becomes more of a homemaker and involved parent. Mom becomes more of a breadwinner. And that can lead to conflict.

Even the most liberated men and women can have trouble adjusting to these new roles. When Joe started helping out around the house, Vicki got upset because she felt she was not adequately fulfilling her duties as homemaker. And when Tina began making more money than Tom, Tom began looking for another job because it upset him to lose his position as primary breadwinner.

Both of these couples will face problems if they do not deal honestly with the essential issue here—self-esteem and identity as they are rooted in cultural stereotypes. Joe needs to find out why Vicki resents his helping around the house. And he also needs to affirm her as still being the person primarily responsible for the household (if that is her desire). Instead of simply taking on certain tasks, Joe would do well to ask Vicki what she wants help with. That way she remains in control of the situation and voluntarily delegates chores to Joe.

Tom solved his problem by changing to a job that paid more than Tina's. But what if he'd been unable to do so? He and Tina would need to look at why making more money is important to Tom—our society associates money with authority, so Tom feels he has lost prestige and authority in the family. Tina can play a big role in helping Tom feel secure in his role despite the shift in income.

All couples, even those who presently fit the traditional stereotypes, would do well to look at the values our society teaches us and ask if they are truly biblical values. Is our identity grounded in a Christian world view, as it should be, or have we allowed our culture to determine how we view ourselves? For example, how many people feel insecure because they do not fit the popular-magazine image of a perfect body? But does that make any difference in Jesus' love for us? No.

Society gives men the role of providers, and that is fine. Someone has to put bread on the table. However, fathers should also nurture their children and be good examples for them. Men can feel caught in the roles they have been assigned. They may feel that they must make such a success of themselves that they cannot turn down a promotion or take a less demanding job even though doing so would allow them to be more attentive parents. And they may feel that they can succeed only at their wives' expense.

A husband who is secure in his identity will be better able to meet his children's needs as well as his wife's. A marriage where both spouses encourage each other to reach their full potential will be a stronger marriage.

Donald Joy, a professor at Asbury Theological Seminary, was asked by *Decision* magazine, "What can a husband do to help his wife become all that God meant her to be?" He responded:

> I think a husband should help his wife dream her dream. . . . Not every woman will want a vocation beyond the household. . . . But they may want to do volunteer work in the church and community. . . . Let the husband say, "I want to be on the cheering stand applauding as you move on." It takes a secure man to do that.

Standing Up for Different Values

After nearly eighteen years of marriage and months of agonizing over the decision, Margaret decided to go back to school. Her childhood dream was to become a nurse, and now she is taking the first steps toward fulfilling that dream. She has the full support of her husband, Paul, and two teenaged daughters. But some of the couple's friends have not been so supportive.

After an evening get-together a friend came up to Paul and asked, "Where's your wife tonight, Paul?"

"Margaret has an assignment due in class tomorrow and she went to the library to work on it," Paul responded.

"You know," said Paul's friend, "I just can't figure out why your wife should want to go back to school now. Your daughters are growing up fast, and I would think she would want to spend as much time as possible with them before they leave home. If she wants to work, why can't she just take some kind of part-time job—one that doesn't require a new degree? If you ask me, I think you'll find that when Margaret finishes her degree she'll be a different person. She may not become a women's libber. She's not the type. But she won't be interested anymore in making a nice home for her family. I've seen it happen before."

How can we counteract such negative judgments? First is simply to listen. Chances are that Paul's friend genuinely believes that bad things happen when women get educated. He is entitled to his opinion. He may be expressing it out of true concern for Paul and Margaret's welfare. So Paul needs to take that into account.

But once we have listened to and understood such statements, we need to respond by informing our friends why we disagree. Paul's friend may not know the reasons behind Margaret's decision to go to school. Once he does know, he may be able to better understand those reasons or at least to see that they are not wrong.

Jesus purposefully violated many of the stereotypes of His day and taught kingdom values instead. For example, one of the prevailing values of Jesus' day was that women, because of their intellectual inferiority, were not to receive religious instruction. In his book *The Upside-Down Kingdom*, Donald Kraybill points out how Jesus included many women among His followers:

> Apparently many women followed Jesus as disciples. As He went preaching the good news of the kingdom of God the twelve were with him and some women—Mary Magdalene, Joanna, Susanna, and many others. These women disciples used their financial resources to help support the disciple group (Luke 8:1-3). The Greek here suggests that they served as deaconesses. By permitting women to travel in public places and to listen to His teaching, Jesus was overturning a number of social norms.[2]

Another prevailing belief in Jesus' time was that menstruating women were unclean. According to Old Testament purity laws, the woman with a hemorrhage described in Mark 5:25-34 was perpetually unclean. Anyone she touched would be made unclean and would have to go through a ceremonial cleansing. By touching the hem of Jesus' garment, the woman defiled Jesus. A typical rabbi would have cursed her and gone immediately to be cleansed. But Jesus invited her to come forward and gave her a special blessing.

By violating stereotypical beliefs, Jesus called attention to the nature of the Kingdom He had come to usher in. Likewise, as the Christian husband and wife become convinced that God is directing them to pursue an unconventional lifestyle, they may, like Jesus, use the opportunity to demonstrate to others the true values of the Kingdom of God.

David arranged with his boss before his son was born to work his usual number of hours in four extra-long days every week so that he could be home on one weekday. Since his wife worked part-time, this arrangement allowed them to minimize the amount of day care they needed. And it gave David a day alone with his baby boy.

Yet sometimes it was hard for David to ignore the flak he got at work. His co-workers would rib him, sometimes cruelly, about his four-day week. They weren't around in the early morning when his day at work began, and they didn't see him go home well after six at night. They felt that it was somehow unfair that he should work four long days instead of five shorter ones.

Yet when he had an opportunity he would share with his co-workers how he felt about family life and his important role as father. Most of these men had never even played with an infant, much less changed or fed one. They wouldn't consider asking for a flex-time arrangement so they could spend time with the family. But David's example may help them to realize their need to be more nurturant fathers.

That's the kind of upside-down value that Jesus espoused. If Christian parents know they are doing what is right in God's eyes, then they should feel secure in their changed roles and identities. They have found identities closer to the biblical norm.

Communicating Love

Issues of identity can affect a marriage indirectly when the partners begin responding to each other out of preconceived roles rather than out of love. When problems like this arise, the key is to talk about them openly with each other.

In chapter six we heard about Mary and Frank whose marriage was in grave difficulty because Mary thought Frank should be helping more around the house. Frank seemed to be taking on the typical male role of distant father. Mary responded by dropping ineffective hints and finally losing her temper altogether.

What might have happened if this couple had sat down—when the problem first arose—and talked it over? As it turns out, Frank wasn't nearly as opposed to helping as Mary thought he was. But because of their extremely poor communication she wasn't aware of his true feelings.

"I've tried helping," Frank said. "But with Mary it's her way or none. She thinks that I'm supposed to jump every time she raises her voice. I've tried helping her out but never once has she so much as said 'thank you, Frank, for pitching in' or 'I love you, Frank, for being a dear'—nothing. And when I ask her for help—well, let's just say I've learned not to ask."

Both Mary and Frank feel victimized. Mary believes that if Frank really loved her he would help out more. Frank feels that if Mary cared for him she would stop nagging him and be grateful.

We might be tempted to lecture them both on Jesus' commandment to love one another as ourselves. But perhaps their problem is that they do not know how to express or communicate that love. In *The Art of Loving* Erich Fromm describes love as having two essential components: understanding and appreciation.[3] Frank and Mary could use a dose of both.

Love as understanding means that we focus on our spouse and identify with him. In the spirit of St. Francis of Assisi, we might pray, "Lord, grant that I may not so much seek to be understood as to understand." To understand another person means, first, trying to identify with that person.

Christ showed his love for us by fully identifying with us. "For we do not have a high priest who is unable to sympathize with our weaknesses, but we have one who has been tempted in every way, just as we are—yet was without sin" (Heb. 4:15).

For husbands and wives, identification might take the form of spending a day in your spouse's shoes. Though this might be impractical, perhaps your spouse could accompany you to work for part of a day and see what kind of pressure—or boredom—you experience there. Likewise, if Mom is the primary caretaker of the children, perhaps Dad could spend a day alone with the kids (while trying to make the meals, do the wash and keep the house clean) to see what she goes through.

Loving through understanding also means listening to your spouse's point of view. When you two were dating, chances are that you hung on each other's words. You couldn't wait to see what new thing you might discover about your loved one. But after five, ten, or fifty years of marriage that novelty has worn off, and you may quit listening altogether to each other.

You need to break old habits by trying new strategies of relating. You could see how many new things you can learn about each other over a romantic dinner. Or instead of assuming that you know what your spouse means by a certain comment, try asking questions and finding the feelings that lie behind a statement. You need to try being more concerned about what your spouse has to say than about getting your own point across.

Loving through appreciation is simple enough. First you have to recognize your spouse's contributions, and then you have to express appreciation for them. Some marriage enrichment seminars have couples make a list of the things they admire about their spouses. Then they have to share those lists with each other.

When was the last time you left your wife a note thanking her for doing the wash? When did you last tell your husband that he did a fine job on the front lawn? When did you compliment her on the way she handled Junior's temper tantrum? Does he know how much you appreciate his doing the dishes after dinner? Have you ever told your spouse that you think she or he is a good person to be married to? Have you said that you like your spouse's sense of humor? ability to express things? calmness? decorating skills? cooking? driving? taste in clothes? We could go on.

If you're out of the habit of appreciating each other, you may have to work hard at first. And if time is at a premium, you may have to make a "date" with your spouse for some private time together to talk. But the more you try to express appreciation, the more things you'll notice to appreciate. And your spouse's whole perception of you may change. Psychologist Carl Rogers has found that when people respond in one way over forty percent of the time, they are perceived as always responding that way.[4] So if you change your percentages, you may change the whole way you are seen—from negative to positive, from cold to warm, from unloving to loving.

Caring Confrontation

Along with appreciating and understanding each other, working couples need to confront each other. Some couples barely talk about anything more significant than the weather. Honesty, feelings, and conflict threaten them so they avoid the possibilities by avoiding all meaningful conversation.

That's easy to do when you are both very busy. Sometimes in the daily rush we can neglect to be honest. It takes time to be honest with each other.

How can you be honest and confront each other without ending up in a harmful dispute? How can working couples practice being open about negative feelings so that those feelings don't build up? The answer is caring confrontation or, as author David Augsburger calls it, "care-fronting." Augsburger's *Caring Enough to Confront* is a brief, easy-to-read manual on fighting fair and getting things out into the open.[5] Every couple should have a copy on their shelves and put its principles into practice. I simply want to summarize three of the most basic aspects of loving confrontation here.

RULE #1: Begin by sharing your feelings. The average person, when angry and upset, expresses those feelings with an accusation: "You act so selfish when you do something silly like . . . " Right off the bat that alienates your spouse.

Instead of using the accusing approach, try focusing on your *feelings:* "I feel angry when . . ." or "I felt humiliated in front of our friends when . . ." Those statements communicate your emotions without assuming that you know your spouse's motivations and without placing blame.

In *The Secret of Staying in Love* John Powell points out what happens when we attempt to ignore our feelings.[6] We end up miscommunicating and talking past one another. In the worst instances, both parties come away convinced that trying to reason with the other is pointless.

RULE #2: Express your feelings in neutral terms. Don't blame your spouse for the way you feel. No one *makes* us feel a certain way. We allow him or her to do that to us. And if we blame our spouse for our feelings, any chance of resolution (and getting that "I'm sorry" that you'd like to hear) will probably disappear.

When Mary attacked Frank for not helping out more around the house, the result was the opposite of what she wanted—Frank withdrew even more. What if Mary had said instead, "Frank, I feel overwhelmed by the number of things I have to do around the house"? Or what if she had simply said, "Frank, lately I find myself getting angry with you a lot and I'm not sure why. I don't want to be angry with you." I recall saying something like that to my wife on one occasion. Rather than turning off the conversation, the remark led to a mutual exploration of the source of the anger and ways to resolve it.

RULE #3: Listen to the feedback you get. We've all known people who are so eager to give us a piece of their mind that they never give us a chance to respond. But genuine communication between husbands and wives requires input from both parties. After you've shared a little, give your spouse a chance to say something. If necessary, ask specific questions to draw out his or her reactions. This way you will be able to understand just what you are communicating. And you will begin to see your spouse's side of the story. (Don't forget: there ARE always two sides.)

Wanting your spouse's feedback is also a very basic way of saying, "You're important to me. That's why I want to know what you think." It will make him or her feel valued.

Making Mutual Decisions

Open communication becomes crucial when important decisions are involved. Our research into marital adjustment discovered some interesting trends. Those couples who had well-adjusted marriages tended to also make decisions on a more mutual basis. Instead of leaving decisions to the husband or major breadwinner, they made decisions together or delegated decisions according to interests and abilities. This was true even in those cases where the couples held to a strong view of the headship of the man in a Christian home. In good marriages, that view of headship did not mean that decisions were made by fiat. They were openly discussed and shared.

There are some decisions in a household which rather naturally break down according to skills and concerns. For example, the person who most often does the vacuuming in the house (be it the husband or wife) is also going to be most concerned about what type of new vacuum is purchased. The one who makes a habit of tinkering with cars and keeping up on the latest information about the new models is going to put the greatest stock in what kind of car is purchased.

In many homes, Dad will research makes and models of cars and choose which one suits the family best. Then Mom will have a major say in what sorts of options are chosen as well as colors. The person who does the budgeting will probably have the most input into decisions about a calculator or savings investment. The point is that the decisions are not made in a rigid manner but a flexible one. Sometimes one person takes the lead, at other times the other does.

Christian author C. S. Lewis, who held a rather traditional view of male/female roles, nevertheless saw the need for flexibility in marriage. In *That Hideous Strength* he said, "Obedience and rule are more like a dance than a drill—specially between man and woman where the roles are always changing."[7]

Some Christians believe in mutual submission between husbands and wives based on Ephesians 5:21. Others believe that the wife is to submit to the husband, based on Ephesians 5:22. But whichever view you take, you must remember that inflexibility has never been very successful where human beings are concerned. That's what Lewis was getting at.

In a formal, ballroom-type dance the man leads. But he does not lead by dragging his wife around the dance floor, barking orders and pushing this way and that. That's not dancing, it's bulldozing. In a dance both partners know what is expected of them; they have learned the steps and their movements are controlled as much by the music (the situation) as by the man's arm on the woman's back. He guides, but they move together or else trip over each other. They progress together as one, each going along with the movements the other is making.

Decisions in marriage should be made with at least that much give-and-take and fluidity. The situation and the needs of the individuals should have more influence on decisions than the rigid structure that society or the church has imposed on the partners. Our research reveals that that kind of mutuality is directly related to marital happiness.

If a decision is not delegated primarily to one spouse or the other, then they need to make it together. I remember overhearing a conversation between a husband and wife. He was showing her a packet of travel brochures he'd just picked up at an agency, and he was obviously excited about the prospect of a different and more adventuresome vacation. But she thought they had already decided what to do.

"We talked last month," she said, "about visiting my parents this year on our vacation."

Apparently this couple had had a conversation about vacation. One of them thought that conversation represented a decision which was discussed and made. The other thought that was a casual conversation which included the possibility of a visit to parents, but came to no conclusion.

That kind of misunderstanding can happen easily in marriage, especially a working marriage where couples have a minimum of time to talk things over. When major issues are involved, the partners need to be clear about how the decision is going to be made, by whom, and when. Once it is made, both must acknowledge it so there can be no mistake that it has been understood.

All this goes back again to the need for open, honest, and clear communication in marriage. If the two of you can talk things over in a calm and giving manner, then chances are there's almost no problem you can't solve between you.

11

GETTING HELP

"When will dinner be ready?"

"In ten minutes."

"Then I'll go put gas in the car now."

"Don't do that! Dinner can be ready in five minutes if you and the boys help."

"Okay, boys, let's set the table."

There was a flurry of activity as the basketball game just happened to be on a commercial break. Two minutes later Mom said, "Come and get your own drinks, please."

"Just a minute, Mom. We want to see if they get another basket."

"Bob, do you want salad?" Mom asked.

No answer. Is this the playoffs? Mom wondered. She decided to go ahead and make salads anyway. It was twenty minutes before everything was on the table.

Typical? Yes. While Dad or the kids may help some with the routines of cooking and cleaning, in most households it is not their responsibility. They help at their convenience, even though Mom works and everyone is supportive of her decision to do so.

Giving moral support and taking on major household responsibilities are two different things. Most husbands have to make a *conscious* effort to help out, as most of the time they just assume that things like meal preparation and cleaning and washing will get done whether they help or not.

Division of Labor

In some ways times have changed dramatically. Lots more mothers are working than a generation ago. And many more people feel that fathers should do more around the house. But statistics show that, when a wife works, the number of hours her husband spends on housework increases only minimally. Working wives still spend nearly three times as many hours as their husbands on housework and child care.[1]

Ways of measuring the amount of hours spent in housework vary from study to study. The highest reported average by husbands is about twelve hours per week. The lowest is about five. But all studies concur that when a wife goes to work the husband's work load at home does not increase significantly. Instead, the woman works more *total* hours each week even though she cuts down some on her household chores.

Full-time housewives tend to spend about fifty-seven hours per week doing tasks around the house. A woman who picks up twenty-five hours of work outside the home might reduce her household chores to about forty-five hours each week, thus increasing her total work load to seventy hours.

The woman who works full-time outside the home may reduce her household chores to thirty hours. But obviously she still has a net increase (to seventy hours or more) in total hours worked in the home and outside. So what's a woman to do? This chapter provides some helpful hints to decrease your work load and increase the amount of help you get from your family.

Five Bad Models

Some women take various bad attitudes towards housework. These ways of behaving and venting feelings do not solve the problem of work overload. Instead, they wreak havoc on family relationships. So don't follow these examples.

1. Superhuman servant. Many women, especially when they first return to work, continue to run the house the way

they've always done. Either they are naive about their own limits of time and energy, or they find it easier to do things the same way rather than trying to be creative about how to do them differently. They don't let children do things for themselves because Mom can do it faster. They don't let Dad or the kids help around the house because they don't do things just the way Mom wants them done. However, because there are only twenty-four hours in a day, this sort of mom will soon change into another variety.

2. Wishful waiter. This type of mom knows what she wants and needs from her family, but she waits for it instead of asking for it. Why? Maybe it's pride. Maybe she expects her husband or children to be able to guess what she needs. That would be nice, but totally unrealistic. He's not a mind reader any more than you are, especially if he is still able to come home to a nice hot supper and a clean house.

3. Passive resister. When the wishfully waiting mother doesn't get what she needs from her family, she may become resistant. She may throw some luncheon meat on the table instead of cooking dinner, or she may stop picking up after others.

If your kids don't pick up their dirty clothes and you just leave them lying in their room, ignoring them and not washing them until they are put in the wash basket, that makes sense. You're forcing your children to face the consequences of their actions—dirty clothes. However, if you refuse to take Jane to her ballet lesson because you are cleaning up the breakfast dishes she left on the table (perhaps because you never told her to clear them), that doesn't make sense. You're taking out your resentment on her, and she's missing out on an important event. Instead, you could leave her dishes on the table and let her know calmly that she will be served dinner when her place is clear. But don't hurt her because she failed to live up to your unspoken expectations.

4. Married martyr. The passive resister and the married martyr (and often the wishful waiter, too) have one thing in

common—a sense of resentment toward their families for not helping more. The passive woman withdraws and refuses to do things. The martyr is different. She continues to do the housework but shows her anger by constantly complaining about how much she is doing. Unfortunately, such an attitude gets her nowhere. It tends to breed defensiveness in her family rather than offers of help.

5. Vengeful retaliator. This is the woman who lets resentment build up, neither passively resisting nor complaining nor expressing her feelings in a constructive way (by caringly confronting family members as we described in the last chapter). Then when something goes wrong, she blows the roof off the house by her explosion of anger.

Things are bound to go wrong sometimes, especially where spouses, kids, and jobs are concerned. When they do, you have to be prepared to deal with your own feelings. Blowing up at your husband or kids by berating them, calling names, criticizing them or hitting them gets you nowhere. Again, it leads to defensiveness, not cooperation.

Instead, you could express your feelings in "I" statements, like "I could scream because the dryer has quit working just when we've got ten loads of wash to do." This way of expressing your feelings without attacking others may get you some volunteers. Dad might even say, "What if Billy loads the wash into the car and he and I take it to the laundromat? You can call the repair service in the morning."

Open Communication

Openly communicating your feelings is probably the best method for getting the help you need. Few spouses are so dense or stubborn as to respond with nothing but a grunt to an honest expression of desperation ("I feel exhausted, and I still have two more rooms to clean before our friends arrive tomorrow; could you help by cleaning the kitchen floor?"). If you don't nag or whine, you may get all the help you ever dreamed of.

You can begin such open communication before you ever go back to work (if you are returning to a job after a number of years away, for instance). A family conference—or at least a talk with your husband—can prevent you from falling into a bad pattern of relating to each other when the going gets tough. Make your husband and older children a part of the decision-making process. They will be affected by the limitations on your time, so they should be able to say in advance how they might like things to work.

Make it clear what kinds of things will change when you begin working. Ask questions: What is more important to you, a super-clean house or time to do things together? Are you willing to iron your own clothes, or will you settle for buying only permanent press? Who is strong enough to take out the trash? What should we do about Rover when he makes a mess? Since dinner will be an hour later, who will take charge of getting snacks ready after school?

Chances are that your problem-solving sessions will come up with solutions that fall into three categories: you will have to try to reduce the amount of housework that needs doing, line up more help from the family, and perhaps hire outside help.

Simplifying Your Housework

There are lots of books on the market full of suggestions for simplifying your housework. And just talking to other working mothers will give you lots of ideas. I just want to list here some general principles that all working mothers should follow.

1. Consider lowering standards. Some women put an extremely high value on having an immaculately clean and organized household. Such women either should not work outside the home or should recognize that doing so will necessitate lowering standards. Just as having a toddler learning to feed herself will force you to stop being so picky about how clean you keep the kitchen floor, so going to work

should also break down some of your cherished norms.

If children are going to help around the house, you have to let them do things their way, not expect them to live up to your standards. Does it matter if the mirror is somewhat streaked after it's cleaned? And what if you or the kids put the underwear in with the dark wash? Does it matter if your unmentionables aren't as white as the ones on TV? If you have company for dinner, will it make a big difference if the three-bean salad was bought at the grocery store deli counter?

One working mom I know only cleans her oven once a year (just before her mother-in-law comes to visit) unless something spills and begins to smoke. After all, she reasons, a stained oven hurts no one. It's not a health hazard. And no one even sees it very often. It's one of those jobs that is somewhat useless but assumed to be on Mom's list of priorities. Why? That's a question you'll have to ask yourself about a lot of household jobs. Do you vacuum your basement regularly? Why? Do you keep Junior's trophy collection on an open shelf where it can collect dust? Why?

2. Cook in bigger batches, and more simply. You shouldn't cook more often, but when you do cook, you should make larger quantities. Another word for leftovers, in my dictionary, is two meals for the work of one. If you're going to make lasagna, make enough for a couple of meals. If home-baked bread is a high priority, then make several loaves at a time. Most food can be easily and successfully frozen, so making two or three batches at a time doesn't mean that you have to eat the same thing for dinner four nights in a row. You just freeze part of it and use it later.

Also, eat more simply. Not every meal has to have several courses. Casseroles are great time-savers because one recipe often includes meat, starch and vegetables. And there are lots of cookbooks these days that offer specially marked recipes that are fast and easy to fix. I like Doris Janzen Longacre's *More-With-Less Cookbook* because it offers good nutrition for less money, doesn't require gourmet cooking techniques, and helps people be good stewards of God's resources.

Many women falsely believe that their families like a lot of fancy meals. Sandra felt that each meal should be a new creation. Her gourmet goulash was a specialty of her house. But when she went back to work, she began cooking much more simply, offering her family hamburgers, chili, and barbecued chicken instead of goulash. To her surprise, everyone was delighted! Her husband cared more about time with her than complicated tastes, and her kids loved the simpler fare.

3. Prevent extra work before it happens. A lot can be done to avoid some of the time-consuming cleaning problems. Dusting, for instance, can be greatly simplified by either putting away the little knickknacks (sports trophies, trip souvenirs, family photos, baby momentos) or putting them in protected places (like glass-enclosed shelves).

Picking up will be easier if you have an organized system of shelves, boxes, file cabinets, etc. Kids toys can be a particular problem. Pegboards, plastic crates and labeled shoe boxes (covered in wrapping paper if you want them to look good) can help simplify the process.

Try to think ahead about possible cleaning problems that will result from how you do something. For example, when the kids go out to play on a muddy day, make sure there are papers by the door for them to put their dirty shoes on when they come in.

Don't buy items that require a lot of care. If your husband wants you to work but insists on buying 100% cotton shirts, maybe it's time he learned to iron. Many working moms never touch an iron except on rare occasions. They buy only permanent-press clothes, and they hang up shirts, dresses, and slacks as soon as the clothes are dry. You can also avoid buying clothes that have to be hand washed or dry cleaned.

Stainless steel tableware, stain-resistant carpeting and no-wax flooring are samples of the many products now available to help cut down on cleaning time.

4. Calculate the time vs. cost factor. Once you begin

working outside the home, your time becomes more precious. Your activities now should be measured in terms of cost effectiveness. When I was working full-time but had no children I used to go to the grocery store an average of two times per week. I did this so that I could take advantage of sales. I would buy peaches on sale at one store and chicken on sale at another. Or I would pick up the specials that a store had at the beginning of the week and then go back for the end-of-the-week specials. Now that I work and have children, I can't do that anymore. By the time I calculated the gas mileage and my time, I found that my extra shopping trips weren't worth the effort.

I found the same thing with coupons. Some women can use them effectively. But I was spending a lot of time clipping coupons, only to forget about them at home or right in the checkout line! Worse yet, I'd buy a new item because I had a coupon for it only to find out that it wasn't nearly as good as the brand I usually buy. Or maybe the discounted price was still more than the store brand.

Sewing is another task that I've found sometimes isn't cost effective. Some women are so efficient at making clothes that they can save lots of money and maybe even time. Other women sew because they want to save money, but they lose lots of time in the process. Would your teenager be happier choosing her own clothes rather than having you make them, even if it means she has fewer clothes? Did you spend hours altering Johnny's pants to fit his younger brother—only to see an equivalent pair of pants on sale for minimal cost? Would Jesse be just as happy with a store-bought Halloween costume as a homemade one? Before doing anything from scratch, ask if it's worth the time.

Many women do things a certain way not because it has to be done that way but because they are trying to live up to false expectations. Linda always tried to make her own clothes when she first got married, even though she also worked full-time and went to school. Linda's mother had always made the kids' clothes as well as her own, and Linda was trying to live up to the standards of her nonworking mom. But Linda found that she was spending huge amounts of time on clothing that she didn't much like when it was finished. When she started buying her clothes on sale instead, she was much happier.

Shopping by catalog can also increase efficiency. If you know exactly what you want, but the store is hard to reach, ordering it and having it shipped (many stores do this at minimal cost) can make a lot of sense.

5. Get organized. Perhaps this is the most basic principle of all. The working mom has to be organized. You don't have time for inefficiency. For example, you should plan shopping trips and errands ahead (or marry someone who loves to shop). Don't rush out as soon as Heather needs a new pair of shoes. Chances are that Timothy is going to need sneakers for gym class. Take them both and get two pairs of shoes at once.

Try to make shopping trips to large malls pay off by making a lot of different stops and purchasing many different items at once—a new shower curtain liner to replace the ripped one, that book you've been wanting to read, underwear for Billy one size larger than he now wears, his school supplies, etc. Some women keep shopping lists according to store and location rather than needs. If the need can wait, let it wait until you need something else at the same place.

By keeping a good supply of canned and other nonperishable food on hand, you can also avoid emergency grocery shopping. Dry milk will do in a pinch. A muffin mix can fill in when you've run out of rolls. Frozen vegetables can be cooked up when the salad fixings run out.

Other ways of being organized are having dental checkups for a couple of family members at the same time, doing errands in between taking the car-pool kids to soccer practice and bringing them home, or doing your mending while helping Ashley with her first term paper.

Getting Your Family to Help

Being organized includes doing things in such a fashion that other people can help you with them. Some women are so disorganized that when Hubby or the kids offer to help Mom can't tell them what to do because she's not sure what needs to be done. If you are going to let your husband and children help around the house, you need to follow some orderly procedures for doing so.

1. Be clear and consistent. In the last chapter we talked about clear and open communication. Those principles apply here. You can't expect your husband to wash the windows if you've never directly asked. And you can't expect your five year old to understand just what the command "clean up your room" entails. You have to make it plain.

Likewise, you must be consistent once you've made a request. If the responsibility for taking out the trash belongs to your teenaged son, then you shouldn't do it yourself when he forgets. The smell and the extra work the next week will bother him, too. They will help him remember to do the job without forgetting.

Or maybe you and your husband have agreed to take turns getting the kids to bed (which can take two hours when you've got three of them!) and cleaning up after dinner. So, when you come downstairs after reading your last bedtime story, only to find the dishes still high in the sink, don't put on an apron and get down to work or verbally attack your husband. Instead, let him take responsibility for his own actions. After he finishes reading the paper and drinking his coffee, he may regret having left the clean-up job till the late hours. Or maybe late evening is when he likes doing such chores. That's his prerogative.

Women are used to being in control of their households. They find it hard to let others alone to do tasks in their own way and on their own time (within the agreed limits). But if you want help, you will have to delegate the tasks fully. That means accepting someone else's standards and way of doing things.

Jack has two teenage sons. He does all their laundry, but the boys are responsible for emptying their pockets and straightening out their clothes before putting them in the hamper. If the clothes come out of the drier inside out, that's the way he hangs them up or leaves them for the boys to fold. He figures the washer didn't turn them inside out. If the boys don't mind inside-out clothes, then why should he? He cuts down on his own work in the process.

2. Offer necessary information. One of the biggest obstacles that kids and husbands face in trying to help out around the house is lack of knowledge.

Perhaps they don't know where you keep seldom-used items like spare vacuum cleaner bags. You might want to let them choose where to put such things, or label drawers and shelves to make it plain.

Perhaps they don't know how to do a certain task. Max tried to be helpful after he and Leslie had their first child and she returned to work. But Leslie found out that the baby was frequently getting ice-cold formula because Max wasn't sure how to warm it up without scalding it or how to check the temperature. She solved the problem by simply having Max watch her one evening. Then when he did it himself and got the formula too hot, she simply thanked him and asked him to put the bottle under cold water for a few seconds. He gradually got the idea.

Letting your husband and kids watch you do something is probably the easiest way to teach them. And you should avoid sounding critical when you correct their procedures. Before you correct, make sure that what they're doing is really bad. Is it harmful in some way, or just different from the way you would do it? Rebecca's husband always washed the dishes using the dishcloth and running water. She was used to using a pan full of soapy water. But after trying to get him to do it her way for a while, she ended up adopting his method. It took no more water and far less time.

Since husbands and kids tend to see household tasks as Mom's responsibility, not theirs, they will quickly give up if they are criticized. You have to be very careful with a child's fragile ego and low tolerance for frustration. When nine-year-old Jake wanted to learn to peel potatoes, Karen decided to give it a try. She set him at the table with a quick lesson on using a peeler. Fifteen minutes later, Jake appeared with a pile of peeled potatoes that were one-quarter their original size.

"The eyes wouldn't come off," Jake said. So he had kept peeling until all the eyes were gone. Fortunately, Karen just started laughing. Then she taught him how to dig out the deep eyes with the peeler or leave them for her to do.

3. Show appreciation. No one wants to be taken for granted, including kids and dads who help around the house. Offer lots of praise and maybe an occasional reward for the help you get. Express gratitude even when a child has been doing a task for weeks or years. Don't begin to take such helpfulness for granted.

You can offer praise for tasks that should become the child's full responsibility. But offer special rewards for chores that are above and beyond the call of duty. If your eight year old loves to play board games, but you haven't got time, try enlisting her help. "If you want to play a game tonight, we can do so only if you finish your dinner quickly and clear the dishes." That offers her a choice and positive consequences for her actions. But you have to be consistent—if she dawdles over her meal or leaves the dishes on the table, then there's no game. You don't have to scold or criticize; you're just not available for checkers.

Buying Services

Even with your family's help and a simplified household, you may find that you would rather pay someone to do some tasks than do them yourself. A recent *Wall Street Journal* carried a story about the booming business in time-savers like take-out restaurants, frozen dinners, disposable baking pans and automatic toilet bowl cleaners. Today's dual-career couples have more money than time, so they use the money to buy time. That's also why microwave ovens, crock pots, and dishwashers are popular.

When buying help or helpful devices, you need to ask a couple of questions to see if the gadget or service is cost effective. First, is the gadget really a time-saver? Things like dishwashers, dryers, and lawn mowers can help you control your work load or end up controlling you. Every time you buy a gadget you are buying something that could break down. And you may also be buying something that is so complicated that it forces you to do a task that your kids might otherwise do.

When I was a child I swept the floor, fed the chickens and collected the eggs, and sliced potatoes. But to provide the same help today, my kids would have to use the vacuum cleaner, go shopping for eggs, and operate a food processor. Those are all complicated tasks. So, is it better to buy the food processor or let the kids learn how to grate and slice with simpler tools? It's up to you.

James Dobson makes a good point that the things we acquire often end up owning us. That's especially true when it comes to extra gadgets or a more affluent life-style. A big yard and fancy gardens are great, until you have to keep them mowed and weeded. The motorbike will save on gas, but is it worth the upkeep for the few months you can use it if you live up north? Will a waffle maker save you time or just force you to make waffles a lot for breakfast? Will you use a crock pot a lot, or does your family dislike stew and soup?

Some time-savers aren't good for you either. In general, the more highly processed foods have less nutritional value. Plain frozen vegetables, for example, are great time-savers and have plenty of vitamins. But frozen entrees tend to be high in sodium and low in nutrition due to overprocessing. Cold cuts often contain a lot of nitrates. So, again, you have to ask if the trade-off is worth it.

A mother who works for small wages also has to be careful that her wages don't get completely used up in paying for day care, prepared foods and other time-savers. You may be paying the cleaning woman more for her help than you make in an hour.

One rule of thumb I use is to buy services that will allow me to spend more time with my kids. But if the kids and I (and Dad) can do the chores together, having fun in the process, then we do it ourselves. One mom says that her three year old loves to clean the mirror, her step stool and her potty while Mom cleans the rest of the bathroom. When Mom is cleaning the kitchen, the toddler tackles the large patio door glass. Window cleaner is nontoxic, so there's almost nothing she can harm, while she gets a big kick out of helping Mommy.

Since many places specialize in cheap and quick oil changes for cars these days, it may not be worth doing it yourself. But if Dad and your teenager enjoy doing it together, it could be a good relationship builder. Family meals at a restaurant can also be a special treat that both gives the family a break from meal preparation and can provide a lot of fun. But you have to measure the cost effectiveness. Chances are that it would make more sense to go to a fast-food or family restaurant for an inexpensive meal than to treat unappreciative kids to a seven-course dinner at the Ritz.

Getting help for a busy mom basically just requires a lot of common sense. The saying goes that the family that plays together stays together. I think that the family that works together stays together, too.

12

CONCLUSION: AT PEACE WITH YOUR CHOICE

SOME FORTY-FIVE YEARS AGO A POPULAR WOMAN'S MAGazine published an article about a housewife named Madge. It described several days in Madge's life, days full of children, housecleaning, cooking, baking, decorating, and seeing friends. Madge coped with crises without a flutter and ran her home with great efficiency.

Reading the article, my former neighbor, Esther Hahn, became disgusted. She decided to write the editors of the magazine protesting their unrealistic picture of motherhood. Her four-page epistle so impressed the editors that they sent a camera crew to her home and ran a full-length article on her.

The pictures showed Esther on a typical day. "Like 95 percent of American housewives," one caption read, "Esther Hahn has no maid. She does all her own cooking, cleaning, laundry, looks after three babies, a husband on the swing shift—and, on the side, runs a gas station." Another picture showed her setting down a load of laundry to answer the service bell at the gas pump, to check oil, pump gas or sell soda pop to a child. Her letter to the editor set the record straight on the life of a typical American housewife.

Dear Editor:

This outburst is the culmination of the effects on me of "One Day After Another" (an article in the May issue of your magazine). It isn't aimed at you especially—but it is time I take something out on someone other than the family.

One evening . . . I told Herb in more or less detail the story of "One Day After Another." At the finish he said: "It sounds like you, hon."

"Yes," I said, "but she stayed nice and sweet all day long. She made corn bread and biscuits and the beds and was so efficient—well, like at ten-thirty she ran up the stairs and the sheets flew and the rugs snapped and the mop ran under the beds and in half an hour she was down with the steps dusted behind her, and just to show how supremely efficient she was, the phone rang *just as she hit the bottom!* And I don't suppose *her* husband ever stood by the ironing board, pantless, at six-twenty in the morning with a horn honking outside, and waited while she ironed his pants. Oh, no, she would have done them the night before, along with the twenty-two shirts. . . ."

Describing her own typical day, Esther concluded her letter: There's the last of the clothes to hang. . . . Now what? I'm dead. But I suppose here's where Madge would take down the first clothes and maybe even start to iron. Well, then she'd clean up the kitchen. She'd never let those oatmeal dishes and stuff sit there this long and she'd wipe up the floor. And start the evening meal. That reminded me—I hadn't even eaten the leftover muffin and coffee and vitamin pill at six-thirty. . . . I got something together on a plate and went to sit . . . a-mulling. Right here is where I decided to do nothing this afternoon (it's two-thirty) but take it out on somebody and maybe get myself straightened out. So—editor, are you still there? Am I the only mommy who isn't like Madge?

Are you the only mommy who isn't like Madge? No. Housekeeping magazines and television can make us feel like we are failures because we come nowhere near their images of motherhood. Our friends and acquaintances can make us feel bad, too. How about all the oohing and aahing that goes on at the church potluck supper over the chocolate mousse that Betty brought? And you are the one who dashed to the grocery to buy two coffee cakes as your contribution.

Not everyone is like Madge. Most of us, working or not, are more like Esther Hahn. But that's okay. It's time we recognized our limitations and accepted them. It's time we made peace with ourselves.

Supermom?

The week before Mother's Day this year seems like a blur to me now. I had to arrange and participate in two car pools for two boys' soccer practices, drive Jason to an orchestra rehearsal, make a court appearance about a traffic accident, make phone calls to harness support for a school board vote on a new district superintendent, attend a curriculum committee meeting for the school district, get to a staff meeting in my husband's office, and go to Paul's preschool for a Mother's Day celebration. All this in addition to the usual demands of the laundry, paying bills, writing my mother, buying groceries, and supervising the boys' piano and cello practice (usually while peeling potatoes or something like that).

It all made me wonder why Mother's Day falls in May. To make a point? Or weren't mothers very busy in the spring when that holiday was instituted?

At the preschool celebration, the children had prepared fruit salad. When I arrived, Paul grabbed me, led me to a chair and ran to dish out some salad for me. He also brought me a drink. I was pleased at how proud he was of his mother. However, I could not quite enjoy that afternoon as much as I had enjoyed it when my firstborn had celebrated Mother's Day at school six years before. Maybe I've had one too many Mother's Days. Or maybe my mind was on work and deadlines. I half wished I didn't have to take time out from my tasks for this kiddie celebration.

Then on Sunday came the clincher. The Mother's Day service at church included pretty bulletins with this inscription:

> Isn't it strange how we elevate careers and lower homemaking to the commonplace? Think how many skills a mother must possess to carry out her duties. She must know something about teaching,

interior decorating, cooking, dietetics, psychology, hygiene, social relations, clothing, household equipment, and a host of things. Still, if a woman teaches someone else's children she is given professional status—a teacher. But if she teaches her own children, she is just a mother. If she does interior decorating she is a career woman; if she decorates her own home, she is just a homemaker. If she takes care of others, she's a nurse; but if she nurses her own children, she's just "mom" doing her job.[1]

That was it. "All right," I thought to myself. "They are trying to tell me to be content with just being mom. After all, there are so many skills I must exercise being a mother that I don't need to be out there showing off my education and my capabilities. Besides, according to them I'm not being a very good mother either. I'm supposed to decorate my home. Well, there are hardly any pictures on my walls and no wallpaper at all. I never sew, and I only bake three times a year—on my sons' birthdays. Even my husband doesn't get a cake (though he's never minded). And when I do bake, I do it out of a box. So, I'm not a professional right now, AND I'm not a good homemaker. What am I?"

Obviously, I am just an ordinary human being. But perhaps I was under pressure to be Supermom that week. That would explain the kinds of reactions I had. How do you avoid such pressures?

Looking for Contentment

Nonworking mothers face discontentment and nonacceptance because they are now in the minority in society. Every day they may hear from friends or relatives (or from inside themselves) subtle messages that say that a woman with no job isn't doing all she should do. They read about working mothers and feel they have to be just like them. They see their friends leaving for work in business suits and wonder why they're staying home with Bobby watching "Sesame Street." They're told that "the hand that rocks the cradle rules the world," but they feel powerless and unappreciated.

Working mothers feel the same. They try to live up to expectations of what a good mother should be, but find they can't possibly fulfill that ideal. They try to focus on the truly important things like peace with God, a healthy marriage and happy children, but there are nagging feelings that their dishes don't sparkle enough or their careers aren't moving fast enough or their children are being neglected.

Mothers face a lot of conflicting expectations that lead to internal conflict. How can you find peace within yourself when you are constantly bombarded with messages that say you should be someone other than you are? Women today face a difficult task in simply finding self-worth among all these contradictory voices.

One of the first things a woman ought to do is to become more realistic about who she is and what she can accomplish. She needs to realize that our society's notions of work, marriage and motherhood are highly romanticized.

A career is supposed to be something you tackle in a superefficient manner, making your way up the corporate ladder without a single misstep or lull.

Motherhood is symbolized by a woman in a apron taking a homemade pie out of the oven and smiling broadly at two muddy cherubs who have just dirtied her newly waxed floor.

Marriage is an ecstatic couple hugging each other and cheering in the bleachers as their daughter takes a bow after a dazzling gymnastics performance.

Those idealized conceptions are lies. The role models that society constructs for us are not real people. Jane Pauley, anchorwoman of NBC's "The Today Show," has been held up by the media as the ideal of working motherhood—a highly successful career woman who is also a mother. But she doesn't even try to live up to her own image. On her refrigerator is reportedly an article about a working mother who said that the way she coped was to stop reading about Jane Pauley.[2] Jane Pauley has also stopped reading about Jane Pauley.

Mothers today—working or not—have to be honest about their limitations. We can't live up to all of society's ideals. Trying to do so produces tremendous stress. Says Helen, a mother of two grown children, "Peace with self requires serious thought about what our underlying goals and motivations are. Honesty with oneself can be a painful process, but it is necessary when one begins to be stressed. I often discover that my stress is self-inflicted. No one cares if my bulletin board stays the same for a month or I bring a store-bought goodie to the Sunday school potluck! But I do, and therein lies the stress."

Women put themselves under a lot of stress when they try to live up to unrealistic expectations and when they say yes to requests instead of no. Saying yes to every request for help is part of trying to fulfill everyone's expectations. When you refuse to recognize your limits, then you keep saying yes.

When you feel overwhelmed by outside concerns that are affecting family life, when you sense that you're on a treadmill, when you can't enjoy time with your kids, then you need to look at how many demands have horned in on your life. You need to start saying no.

Will the others on the PTA really think less of you if you don't contribute to the bake sale? Are you truly disappointing God if you turn down an invitation to sponsor the youth group even though you don't feel you can relate well to teens? Will your husband actually lose his job if you don't show up at the company dinner to benefit the March of Dimes?

Saying no is hard to do when you are trying to win acceptance from society. But perhaps it is time that society began accepting women in *all* their roles.

Time for Acceptance

That quote in the church bulletin about motherhood really bothered me when I read it on Mother's Day. But when I reread it later I had to agree with it. I had not read the sentence: "Yes, motherhood demands the skills of many and, unfortunately, receives the recognition of few."

"That's it!" I thought. "That's why it's so hard to find contentment. The problem is not with motherhood but with the way society treats mothers."

Susan and Jason were mentioned in chapter three. They are both doctors, but Susan has not worked since their first child became autistic. Recently, when son Randy turned fourteen, she began checking into renewing her license. But that required substantial additional training because she had been out of medicine for so long. And there were no training programs near their home where Jason has a successful practice.

When Susan could not find a training program nearby, Jason could have simply told her to be content with what she has. After all, she has accomplished much as a wife and mother. She doesn't need to accomplish anything as a doctor. But Jason didn't say that. Instead, he offered to leave his practice and take a job near a medical school. It was important to him that she be able to find contentment in her own way. Susan declined his offer, but found it easier to be content knowing that she had been given a choice.

Jason and Susan are unusual. Jason appreciates his wife's sacrifices so much that he was willing to make great sacrifices himself in order to give her what she wanted.

Tom and Jean are also unusual. When Tom's new business failed, they were left with debts of almost fifty thousand dollars. Jean had to go to work then, arranging for their children to go to a friend's house after school. Tom found work at first only part-time. Later, when he found steadier work, they reexamined their lives.

They could keep up with daily expenses using just Tom's salary, but they couldn't begin to pay back the debts. Nevertheless, they decided that their family came before the debts. They also wanted to be more active in church. So Jean cut back her work to one day per week, and they arranged for their debts to be repaid more slowly.

Tom and Jean are unusual in having a strong sense of what they want to do with their lives. They have taken steps to do it and are happier because of their decision.

Some mothers choose to work. Others choose to stay home. What all mothers these days need is not a lot of arguments promoting or berating working motherhood. Instead, they need support for making the right decision for themselves and their families—to work or not to work. For Christians, that support should come from the Christian community and from their relationship to God. If we are doing what is right in God's eyes, then we need not worry about society.

Many of us have an unconscious need to prove to ourselves that we are worthy people. In my case, that took the form of a strong ambition to become a doctor. The doctor is at the top of the prestige scale in many societies. The medical missionary also used to be among the most admired people in Christian circles. (Now, I'm told, it's the successful Christian businessman.)

From age ten, I worked hard towards the goal of entering medical school someday. It was not till my senior year of college, after my applications were filed and interviews completed, that I realized what was behind my drive.

A spiritual crisis brought me to the realization that I'll never find contentment in my own achievements. Instead, I am worthy—infintely worthy—because of God's love for me. He valued me enough to give up His Son for me. Why, then, would I need to find acceptance—from myself, from society, or even from the church—in what I do?

Freedom and Responsibility

The emphasis today in the women's movement is on rights. We have rights to fulfilling jobs, good marriages, happy children, everything. But the Christian life does not focus on rights. Our focus as believers is on Christ. If we constantly wonder, "What am I missing out on?" we mar our ability to model ourselves after him "Who, being in very nature God, did not consider equality with God something to be grasped, but made himself nothing, taking the very nature of a servant . . . and became obedient to death—even death on a cross!" (Phil. 2:6-8).

Nevertheless, while we ought not to focus on our rights, most of us do have freedom to make certain choices. We don't necessarily have a right to a fulfilling job or a husband who makes enough money to support the whole family, but we may have the freedom to choose to be a mom who works outside the home or not.

As we exercise our freedom of choice, we ought to ask ourselves two questions: are we allowing others the same freedom we have? and what is our goal in the choices we make?

When we treat judgmentally those who have made choices different from ours, we are taking away their freedom. Being a working mother or an at-home mother is not dictated by the Ten Commandments. Nor is it a necessary condition of our salvation. It falls squarely into that part of life over which God has allowed us to use our discretion. In using that discretion we grow as moral beings. We should encourage others to likewise make their choices according to Scriptural principles applied to their own particular circumstances. We should affirm the choices that others make even when they differ from our own.

Of course, because we live in a fallen world, our choices will never be completely unconstrained. Amanda, for example, did not want to work. But she had worked ever since she married Ken. That's because Ken did not like the idea of being the sole supporter of her and their two children. Even though his salary could provide a modest living, he wanted extras like money to spend on expensive hobbies. So Amanda works to pay for groceries and for her own spending money.

Amanda wasn't completely free to choose not to work. The

other responsibilities in her life limited her. That's the way it is for most of us—we make trade-offs. If we're not careful those trade-offs can make us bitter, so we need to have the attitude of Christ toward all that we do.

The apostle Paul encouraged this attitude in the believers at Ephesus, some of whom were slaves. Without condoning slavery, he told them, "Slaves, obey your earthly masters with respect and fear, and with sincerity of heart, just as you would obey Christ. Obey them not only to win their favor when their eye is on you, but like slaves of Christ, doing the will of God from your heart. Serve wholeheartedly, as if you were serving the Lord, not men, because you know that the Lord will reward everyone for whatever good he does, whether he is slave or free" (Eph. 6:5-8).

Even if your freedom to choose a life-style is limited, your freedom to choose your attitude is not. Who are you trying to serve? Are you serving society, trying to live up to Madison Avenue's image of the career woman or the nurturing mother? Are you serving your own selfish motives? Or are you making yourself available to do the work God has for you, whatever it may be at any particular stage in life?

A Sense of Calling

So—as Christians we have the freedom to choose whether to work outside the home or not. But we also have to examine why we are doing what we do.

As Christians our motive should be to use all the talents God has given us and to encourage others, including our spouses, to do the same. Dr. Josif Ton, former Baptist pastor in Romania now in exile in the U.S., tells this story about his wife. When the Communist authorities threatened to send him to labor camp if he continued to preach, he became concerned for his own safety and that of his family. He wanted to accept the government's offer of another job if he would stop preaching.

But his wife would not let him. She challenged him to

remain faithful to God's call on his life. She reminded him that they had committed themselves to obeying and trusting God. Finally Josif went to the authorities and told them he would continue preaching as long as he could. Surprisingly, they did not send him to labor camp, but they took away his license to preach. He continued to preach without a license until they banished him from the country.

While in exile, he founded the Romanian Missionary Society which distributes Christian literature. Through it, the Christian message has reached more people in Romania than ever before.

Tom's wife did not consider her rights to companionship and safety. She did not treat her husband as someone who must support her and their family. Instead, she saw that he had a calling and that she as his wife must support that calling even if it threatened her own welfare.

Today we need husbands and wives, co-workers and friends, extended family members and church members who will support our calling from God, whatever that may be. Most of us will never face such a dramatic choice as did Josif Ton and his wife. But life is the sum total of little choices made each day. The willingness of a husband to shoulder his fair share of parenting responsibilities, to listen, and to avoid adding to the stresses his wife feels, can make all the difference in how a woman responds to God's call on her life.

What do we mean by a call from God? Two common misconceptions predominate in the Christian community. One is that God only calls people to "spiritual ministry," not secular tasks. Many in the church believe that pastors, chaplains and others in "full-time Christian service" are called by God but mothers, fathers, plumbers, pilots, teachers and welders are not. This is wrong. God calls each of us to serve Him in everything we do—washing dishes, answering phones, changing diapers, typing papers, making meals, removing a diseased kidney, mowing the lawn, fixing a carburetor, doing the wash, or processing a bank statement. Whatever God gives us to do we are to "do it all for the glory of God" (I Cor. 10:31).

The second common misconception, one that has been a focus of this book, is the idea that God mainly calls women to be homemakers. That idea narrows the freedom God has given us in Christ. God has not specified what women must do. The Bible recounts stories of women in many different walks of life who were used by God. Deborah, a prophetess and judge, went to war for the Israelites (Judg 4). Lydia was a cloth dealer. Her home became a base for Paul and Silas and other Christians in Philippi (Acts 16). Priscilla and Aquila, a married couple, were tentmakers who were also involved in evangelism and discipleship along with Paul (Acts 18).

What is God's calling for you? In making our choices, we must be sure that we are listening to God, not to our own preconceptions. Our call may take us outside the approval of our church or our friends. They may believe that we are not following God's will even when we are.

In the church we admire those who fit our preconceived notions of serving God. For example, we admire the missionary couples that send their children away to boarding school for months at a time so the parents can minister in remote parts of the world. But does the same admiration apply to those who leave their children for shorter periods in order to pursue the call God has given them in another kind of work?

Lise remembers a clear sense of calling received at a young age to become a doctor. Later experiences confirmed that call. When she met Jon in college, she found that he shared a deep sense of calling and an interest in health care. He also shared her belief that she should become a doctor. They married and took turns getting further training and working.

When they had a child, Jon started his own business so he could have flexible hours and be home a lot to care for their preschooler. Lise continued medical training and for three years commuted six hours to school each week, returning home to the family on weekends.

That was a difficult time for them. They did not have the support of many friends or the Christian community. Like the missionaries, Lise was away from her child—though only temporarily—because she was fulfilling her calling from God. But that was not accepted by many people. The couple succeeded during this hard period only because they both kept their calling firmly in mind.

God has a call for each of us. Some of us are called to marry while others are not. Some of us are called to give our lives to our children as parents, while others are not. Some of us are called to paid employment while others will give themselves in volunteer work, hospitality, friendship or charitable service.

God calls each of us to be good stewards—of our spouses, our children, our money, our time, and our talents. That's what this book is all about—finding our calling and carrying it out. Making choices. Fulfilling God's claim on our lives. Do you have a sense of God's claim on your life? What are you doing today with the things the Master has entrusted to you?

NOTES

Introduction

1 *Redbook,* August 1986, p. 78.
2 *McCall's,* May 1985.

Chapter 1: Women and Work

1. From H. Hayghe, *Monthly Labor Review,* February 1986, pp. 43-45.
2. *Time,* 22 June 1987, p. 60.
3. Ethan Allen survey cited in *Parentguide,* November 1986, p. 12.
4. *Redbook,* August 1986, p. 79. This is hardly a surprising statistic since one would expect people to justify their own life-style.
5. Ethan Allen survey, *Parentguide.*
6. William R. Johnson and Jonathan Skinner, "Labor Supply and Marital Separation," *American Economic Review* Vol. 76, no. 3, pp. 455-69.

Chapter 2: Should Mothers Have Jobs?

1. Reported in Statistical Abstracts of the United States, 1986.

Chapter 3: Children or Career?

1. Fred Arnold and James T. Fawcett, *The Value of Children:*

A *Cross-National Study,* vol. 3 (Honolulu: East-West Population Institute, East-West Center, 1976).

2. Louis Genevie and Eva Margolies, *The Motherhood Report: How Women Feel About Being Mothers* (New York: Macmillan, 1987).

3. Ibid.

4. *Newsweek,* 1 September 1986.

5. Hakon Torjesen, *The Househusband* (Eden Prairie, Minn.: The Garden, 1979).

6. Quoted in *The New York Times Magazine,* 7 December 1986, p. 160.

7. Joan Beck, "Women Shooting for CEO Jobs May Pay Personal Cost," *Chicago Tribune,* 24 May 1987.

Chapter 4: Is Money a Reason to Work?

1. Quoted in Barbara Basler, "Putting a Career on Hold," *The New York Times Magazine,* 7 December 1986, p. 160.

2. Thomas Espenshade, *Intercom,* September 1980.

3. Lawrence Olson, *Intercom,* November/December 1982.

4. T. Berry Brazelton, *Working and Caring* (Reading, Mass.: Addison-Wesley, 1985).

Chapter 5: What Happens to Your Kids?

1. *Redbook,* August 1986, p. 78.

2. *Newsweek,* 1 September 1986.

3. Peter Barglow, Brian E. Vaugh, and Nancy Molitor, "Effects of Maternal Absence Due to Employment on the Quality of Infant-Mother Attachment in Low-Risk Sample," *Child Development* Vol. 58 (1987): pp. 945-54.

4. Brazelton, *Working and Caring,* p. 61.

5. Summaries of the controversy can be found in *Time,* 22 June 1987; *The Wall Street Journal,* 3 March 1987; and *Psychology Today,* February 1986.

6. Gerald Leslie, *The Family in Social Context* (New York: Oxford, 1982), p. 536.

7. Kristin A. Moore, and Isabel V. Sawhill, "Implications of

Women's Employment for Home and Family Life," in *Women and the American Economy,* ed. Juanita M. Kreps (Englewood Cliffs, N.J.: Prentice-Hall, 1976), pp. 102-122.

8. John Guidubaldi et al., "Maternal Employment and Child Adjustment: Results of a Nationwide Survey," paper presented at the 94th Annual Convention of the American Psychological Association, Washington, D.C., August 1986.

9. Kristin A. Moore, and Sandra L. Hofferth, "Women and Their Children," in *The Subtle Revolution: Women and Work,* ed. Ralph E. Smith (Washington, D.C.: The Urban Institute, 1980).

10. U.S. Department of Labor, *20 Facts on Women Workers,* 1980.

11. *Newsweek,* 1 September 1986. See also Moore and Hofferth, "Women and Their Children."

12. Sandra Scarr, *Mother Care/Other Care* (New York: Basic Books, 1984).

13. Moore and Sawhill, "Implications of Women's Employment for Home and Family Life," in *Women and the American Economy,* ed. Juanita M. Kreps (Englewood Cliffs, N.J.: Prentice-Hall, 1976), p. 114.

14. J. Ross Eshleman, *The Family: An Introduction* (Boston: Allyn & Bacon, 1981), p. 123.

15. Guidubaldi et al., "Maternal Employment and Child Adjustment."

Chapter 6: What Happens to Your Marriage?

1. The study consisted of a randomly selected sample of married parents residing in Wheaton, Illinois. The study is currently being prepared for publication.

2. W. W. Meade, "Changing Men, Changing Marriage," *Working Woman,* November 1986, pp. 170-71, 252.

3. Reuben Hill and Robert Becker, quoted in Strong et al., *The Marriage and Family Experience,* 2nd. ed. (New York: West Publishing, 1983), p. 185.

4. Steven L. Nock, *Sociology of the Family* (Englewood Cliffs,

N.J.: Prentice-Hall, 1987), p. 160.

5. Johnson and Skinner, "Labor Supply and Marital Separation," *American Economic Review* Vol. 76, no. 3, pp. 455-69.

Chapter 7: True Guilt and False

1. Carol Gilligan, *In a Different Voice* (Cambridge: Harvard Univ. Press, 1982).

2. John White, *Parents in Pain* (Downers Grove, Ill.: InterVarsity Press, 1979), pp. 180, 81.

3. Cited in Neala S. Schwartzberg, "Call Me Supermom," *Parents,* March 1986, pp. 79-82.

4. Ibid.

5. Ibid.

6. Jeanne Bodin and Bonnie Mitelman, *Mothers Who Work: Strategies for Coping* (New York: Random House, 1983), pp. 36-38. See also *Psychology Today,* August 1976, p. 29.

Chapter 8: Finding Substitute Child Care

1. *The Wall Street Journal,* 30 March 1987.

2. Brazelton, *Working and Caring,* p. 138.

3. *The Wall Street Journal,* 12 February 1987.

4. Earl A. Grollman and Gerri L. Sweder, *The Working Parent Dilemma* (Boston: Beacon Press, 1986).

Chapter 9: Shared Parenting

1. Grollman and Sweder, *Working Parent Dilemma.*

2. Ibid., p. 29.

3. Ibid., pp. 13, 14.

4. Ibid., p. 15.

5. S. G. Timmer, J. Eccles, and K. O'Brien, "How Children Use Time," in *Time, Goods and Well-Being,* ed. F. Thomas Juster and Frank P. Stafford (Ann Arbor: University of Michigan Institute for Social Research, 1985).

6. Scarr, *Mother Care/Other Care.*

Chapter 10: Nurturing the Working Marriage

1. White, *Parents in Pain*, p. 108.
2. Donald B. Kraybill, *The Upside-Down Kingdom* (Scottdale, Pa.: Herald Press, 1978), pp. 243-45.
3. Erich Fromm, *The Art of Loving* (New York: Harper & Row, 1956).
4. Cited in David W. Johnson, *Reaching Out: Interpersonal Effectiveness and Self-Actualization* (Englewood Cliffs, N.J.: Prentice-Hall, 1972), p. 129.
5. David Augsburger, *Caring Enough to Confront* (Glendale, Calif.: Regal Books, 1973).
6. John Powell, *The Secret of Staying in Love* (Niles, Ill.: Argus Communications, 1974).
7. C. S. Lewis, *That Hideous Strength* (New York: Macmillan, 1946), p. 149.

Chapter 11: Getting Help

1. Heidi Hartman, "The Family as the Locus of Gender, Class, and Potential Struggle," SIGNS 6, no. 3 (Spring 1981); Donna Hodgkins Berardo, Constance L. Shehan, and Gerald R. Leslie, "A Residue of Tradition: Jobs, Careers, and Spouse's Time in Housework," *Journal of Marriage and the Family* Vol. 49 (May 1987), pp. 381-90.

Chapter 12: Conclusion

1. Leslie B. Flynn, "Mother," American Tract Society.
2. *Reader's Digest*, July 1987.